DEAD TOWNS
AND LIVING MEN

BEING PAGES
FROM AN ANTIQUARY'S NOTEBOOK

BY

C. LEONARD WOOLLEY

HUMPHREY MILFORD
OXFORD UNIVERSITY PRESS
LONDON EDINBURGH GLASGOW NEW YORK
TORONTO MELBOURNE CAPE TOWN BOMBAY CALCUTTA
1920

CONTENTS

	PAGE
Introduction	1
Egypt	8
Italy	46
Carchemish	74
Haj Wahid—and Others	96
The Kaimmakam of Birijik	146
A Chief of the Kurds	178
Naboth's Vineyard	222
Aleppo	236

LIST OF ILLUSTRATIONS

	TO FACE PAGE
The Author and T. E. Lawrence at Carchemish .	*Frontispiece*
Faras: Digging up Meroïtic Graves	28
Faras: The Coptic Monastery on the Hill . . .	30
Teano: The Roman Baths during Excavation . .	47
Mask of a River-God from the Teano Baths . . .	53
Statue of Cupid from the Teano Baths . . .	55
Group of Workpeople at the Baths, Teano . . .	59
The Enceinte Wall of La Civita in the Valley of the Sabato, showing the Gateway on the left . . .	72
Carchemish: General View of the Excavations (1913) .	76
Carchemish: The Expedition House from the City Wall .	78
Sketch Plan of Carchemish	81
Clearing Sargon's Fort on the Top of the Acropolis Mound .	82
Carchemish: The Gateway of the Processional Entry .	84
Carchemish: The Long Wall of Sculpture enclosing the Temple Court below the Great Staircase . .	86
Carchemish: Sculptured Slab at the Foot of the lower Palace Staircase	89
Carchemish: The Royal Buttress	91

viii DEAD TOWNS AND LIVING MEN

	TO FACE PAGE
Carchemish: The Temple Court	93
Carchemish: The East Wall of the Processional Entry	94
Carchemish: The Living-Room in the Expedition House	99
A Group of Workmen	116
The Head-Men	122
"Yallah!"	132
A Fifth-Century Mosaic	148
Busrawi (in the Centre) with two Minor Chiefs	194

INTRODUCTION

THE archæologist is no longer quite the *rara avis* that he was, nor does his profession necessarily evoke the idea of broad-rimmed spectacles and a snuffy waistcoat (though, to be sure, when Lawrence and I were joining the Survey party in Sinai the R.E. officer in charge wrote disgustedly to an assistant that two doddering greybeards from the British Museum were descending on them!); but it is still so far out of the common run as to excite a half-amused interest and to retain a certain glamour. "What on earth made you choose such a line?" "Did you have to go through a special training for it?" These are the more serious questions generally put to one, while with the gentler sex it is rather, "It must be wonderfully exciting, isn't it?" and "Do you really dig yourself?" and "What was the best thing you ever found?" I am afraid that ladies are sometimes disappointed to learn that the archæologist does not, as a rule, wander round shouldering pick and spade to dig out treasures unaided, like some errant prospector after gold; they find it far less dramatic that he should merely run a gang of paid labourers, and devote his time less to manual toil than to the humdrum task of taking notes and making photographs, and "the best thing" that you have found—even supposing you could name it—would probably appeal to them far less than many another thing to which you yourself have given but little thought. There *is* a romance in digging, but for all that it is a trade wherein long periods of steady work are only occasionally broken by a sensational discovery, and even then the real success of the season depends, as a rule, not on the rare "find" that loomed so large for the moment, but on the information drawn with time and patience out of the mass of petty detail which the days' routine little by little brought to light and set in due perspective.

Sometimes, it is true, the archæologist must become literally a digger; gangs have to be trained, and raw hands must be shown by example how objects are to be unearthed without damage, how the pickaxe should become a sensitive thing to distinguish what is still hidden from the eye, how for delicate work knife and brush must be called into play; but when once the lesson has been taught, it is best to leave the men to do their own work with the tools which they understand far better than you do, though at first they may have to use them in unaccustomed ways, and the archæologist should himself be free to deal with things already found and with the general direction of his men.

And for his work there is no special training other than experience—experience begun, if possible, under a good teacher who can train him in proved methods and show him how results should be presented. An apprenticeship in a museum is of great assistance, for there one learns more about the preservation of objects than field-work alone can teach, and becomes familiar with a wider range of antiquities than any one excavation can produce. But no form of knowledge which the beginner in field-work may possess will fail to help him somewhere. History of all sorts, and in particular the history of the country wherein he works, languages, acquaintance with museum shelves, and with the published records of other diggings, photography, chemistry, carpentering and engineering, geometry and surveying, medicine and accounting, botany, natural history, ethnology—there is nothing that will not be of use; and though none of us can lay claim to all the attainments of the ideal archæologist, none need be afraid that any branch of study will be wasted. Above all things, the fieldworker must be able to manage men.

If, then, there is no special course for the archæologist, and seeing that I do not possess one-quarter or one-tenth of the qualities of the Admirable Crichton that he should be, why, I am asked, did I choose such a profession? The dedication of this book will, I hope, excuse a brief note of autobiography by way of answer. The fact is, I did not choose it; it was chosen for me.

Towards the end of my last year at New College I was honoured with an invitation to wait upon the Warden in his lodgings at 10 A.M. Wondering which of a good many things might be the reason, and hoping it was not most of them, I duly presented myself in as non-committal a frame of mind as I could assume; but I was not at all prepared for the turn the conversation took.

"Ah, Mr. Woolley," began the Warden. "Quite so. I think that when you came up to Oxford you had every intention of taking Holy Orders?"

I murmured something unintelligible and waited.

"And I am afraid that you have quite abandoned the idea."

"Oh, rather," I said hurriedly; "yes, quite, Mr. Warden, quite given it up."

"And what do you propose to do?"

"Well," I answered, "I want to be a schoolmaster; I've done a little at odd times and like it awfully, so I think of going in for it permanently."

"Oh, yes; a schoolmaster, really; well, Mr. Woolley, *I* have decided that you shall be an archæologist."

There was no more to be said. I had, like many other undergraduates, gone to lectures on Greek Sculpture and on the beginnings of Greek civilization, but, like them, had had no intention of taking up such things very seriously. Now that the Warden had decided my fate for me, I went off to Germany and France to get up modern languages, and though the immediate scheme fell through, and I did after all resort to schoolmastering, yet Canon Spooner was stronger than circumstance, and within a year I was back at Oxford as assistant under Sir Arthur Evans, then Keeper of the Ashmolean Museum. So I can plead that if I fall short indeed of the manifold requirements of a field archæologist, I did not temerariously thrust myself into that select company, but did meekly as I was told.

And if I now embark upon a book other than that somewhat arid record of things found, by which the modern digger justifies his claim to be a man of science, it is because the digger aforesaid does not go about with a spade on his bent shoulders and his eyes fixed on the ground, and does not spend all his spare time in the dust of museum cellars or on the library ladder. His work takes him far afield, and he gets to know countries and the ways of men from a point of view other than that of the tourist or of the resident official. He is thrown into close touch with just that class—the labourer and the country villager—which is least obvious to most; he penetrates into the less-known parts, becoming more familiar with some obscure town or lonely hamlet than with the social centres that attract the student or the casual visitor; he speaks the language of the people, and because of duties towards them freely shouldered becomes in a measure a sharer of their life and of their confidence. In this book, then, archæology takes a minor part, and the stories deal mainly with things seen or done in work's interludes. The work goes on meanwhile — that is the background of it all — but there are free times when one can study, as indeed one must study if the work is to go well, the men who are busy with pick and spade and basket, their characters and the conditions of their being: there are the incidents that arise out of the work without being precisely of it, serious happenings and laughable; there is about one the atmosphere of the historic past and of the living world wherein that history was made; and if out of all this a man cannot reap a harvest for the widening and the delight of his own soul he must be a purblind creature and poorly suited to his task: for him and through him there can be no stirring and murmur of new life in the valley of dry bones where he works. But whether out of this harvest he can make bread to offer to those who have asked only stones of him is another question, and should he fail therein it is less his want of skill that merits blame—for after all the archæologist need not be an artist—than his rashness in trying; he should have stuck to his last so far as writing goes.

Probably I should never have started on this book had I not found myself a prisoner of war, with many hours of enforced idleness to overcome. The war brought the archæologist out in a new light, and his habit of prying about in countries little known, his knowledge of peoples, and his gift of tongues, were turned to uses far other than his wont. In Egypt alone there were half-a-dozen of us attached to the Headquarters Staff; in Mesopotamia, in the Greek islands and at Salonica, there were intelligence officers and interpreters who had graduated in archæology, and the discovery that what had seemed the mere stock-in-trade of one's profession could thus find wider scope made one regard it as possessing maybe some value of its own. So, having nothing better to do in Castamuni, I have tried to set in order the scrap-book of a digger for "antikas." The incidents of our work at Carchemish take most space, for there we were in less-known parts, and life was more amusing; but though the book deals with the lighter side of things — a mere stringing together of anecdotes and sketches of individuals — and is very far from being a serious study of social questions, I yet hope to have given in these chapters some idea of native life between Aleppo and the Taurus, and of what Turkish rule meant there. The War will without doubt bring great changes to Syria, affecting most just those conditions with which we were most familiar, and therefore some interest may attach to anything which illustrates the old order. So I have not allowed later experiences to colour my descriptions; as a prisoner of war I have seen enough of Turkish brutality towards my countrymen to justify any attack upon the Turks, however bitter, but the stories in this book are told as they happened, with no comment other than I should have made before ever war was declared, and the resulting picture, so far as it goes, is a truthful one.

But these are mountainous birth-pangs, and, after all, I have no wish to be taken very seriously.

KEDOS, 1918.

EGYPT

For any one who would be a field archæologist Egypt is the best of schools. So much work has been done in the Nile Valley that its archæology is well known now, and the beginner can check his results at almost every turn by the published records of his predecessors: there is perhaps less scope for the imagination, but minute observation and the most painstaking method are essential if he is, on the one hand, to avoid palpable mistakes, and, on the other, to add his share of detail to our knowledge of the period with which he deals. Moreover, he can always start under the direction of an experienced digger, and, joining one of the expeditions annually at work in Egypt, has under him workmen already trained, so that he can devote himself to supervision and to his records without need to worry over the education of unskilled labour. Lastly, he is in a settled and civilized country where the authorities will help instead of hindering him, and he can therefore pursue his task without distraction.

With all these advantages, however, he will find his days fully occupied. In the dry soil of Egypt objects are for the most part so well preserved that, if the site be at all a rich one, he is liable to be overwhelmed with the mass of antiquities which come to light and have to be studied and recorded, cleaned or mended, drawn or photographed. In my own experience of cemetery-digging in Egypt a gang of thirty workmen will keep one well employed, and though I have worked on tomb-sites with double that number it was a strain which, I think, was not without its effect on the quality of the work.

I shall always be thankful, therefore, that I served my apprenticeship in Egyptology, though I had no intention of specializing in that branch, nor was qualified to do so. I am convinced that nobody ought to undertake field-work in the Nile Valley unless he have at least a fair knowledge of Egyptian, and can decipher sufficiently for his own guidance the hieroglyphic inscriptions which he may find. I never had that knowledge, and cannot forget how great a drawback was my ignorance when I was digging some XIXth Dynasty graves at Anibeh in Nubia. Many of these graves belonged to members of a single family, descendants of one Penno, who was governor of the city of Ma'am under Thothmes III. Penno's own rock-cut sepulchre, the only known example of its kind between the first and second cataracts, lies on the edge of the upper desert: the painted reliefs of the main chamber were well preserved, and it is a grievous pity that they were ruined in 1910 by a plundering dealer. The shaft-tombs of his descendants, cut in the lower plateau, contained inscriptions and named *ushabti* figures which would have enabled me to arrange all my finds in a series accurately dated by generations, and it would have been of the utmost use to do this on the spot instead of months later when the objects were scattered between different museums; but I could not read the hieroglyphics, nor was there any one to help me, and my work suffered in consequence.

I was fortunate, therefore, in that nearly all my digging was done on non-Egyptian sites. These lay between Korosko and Halfa, beyond the limits of Egypt proper, and, for the most part, yielded the remains of a civilization unknown before, whose language, it being as then undeciphered, the field-worker could be excused from knowing.

It was at Karanog, on the outskirts of the Nubian village of Anibeh, that Dr. MacIver and I dug the first big Meroïtic cemetery on record, and that season was exciting enough.

A certain number of inscriptions in mysterious characters had long been noted in Nubia or as coming from that country, a few painted pots, of which neither the date nor the place of finding was assured, had made their way into museums or private collections, and there was always the sensational treasure of enamelled jewellery which Ferlini claimed (and I think truthfully claimed) to have found in the pyramids of Gebel Barkal in Dongola; but the character of the civilization which had produced these things, even if all were to be assigned to the same civilization, as many refused to credit, remained a problem. Great was our joy, therefore, when, attracted to the spot by traces of brickwork resembling that which had marked the tiny plundered graveyard of Shablûl, discovered by him the season before, MacIver and I set to work at Karanog, and from its crowded graves, brick-vaulted or burrowed in the hard mud, recovered the whole art and industry of a new race. There were inscribed and painted gravestones and tomb-altars by the hundred, bronze vessels, some of Greek workmanship, and some engraved with pictures or patterns of a strange and local style, implements and weapons, woven stuffs, glass vessels and beads, and caskets of wood and ivory, and, above all, pottery, pottery in bewildering quantities, much of it painted in bright colours and with designs now delicate and now grotesque. I can well recall how enthusiastic we were over each fresh discovery, and how proud of the really wonderful collection that resulted from our season's work; but I must confess that when we began finding tombs of the same sort at Halfa, a year later, our enthusiasm was not so keen, and when I dug some hundreds more of the same type at Faras in 1911 it was difficult to pump up any pleasurable emotion. Whether these finds belong to the earlier Candace Empire, which was driven out of Nubia by Petronius, the General of Augustus Cæsar, or whether they represent, as most of the Karanog things do, the later Blemmyan occupation which, up to Justinian's time, so worried the frontier of Roman Egypt, the damping fact remains that we have to deal with something of purely local interest. The whole Meroïtic civilization was but a backwater, remarkable as an isolated phenomenon in African history, but contributing nothing to the general stream of culture and of art. To most of us an ancient civilization appeals in so far as it has directly or indirectly influenced that of to-day ; but Meroïtic art was sterile and died with the power of the people that produced it. Much, therefore, as I enjoyed those early days of discovery, when *omne ignotum pro magnifico* was splendidly true, I should be more than loth to return to the same field ; and heartily relieved was I, at Faras, to leave the Meroïtic cemetery for the little Ist Dynasty graveyard and the frescoed churches of the Christian town.

For our work in Nubia we brought with us a gang of trained diggers, fellahîn from the village of Kuft, in Middle Egypt, but we also raised a certain number of recruits from the neighbourhood. Nubia is, properly speaking, the home of the Berberines, but the Berberine devotes himself to domestic service in Egyptian towns, is cook, butler, bottle-washer or chamberman, and hates manual work out of doors ; all our local men were negroes who during Mahdist times or in the earlier years of our reoccupation had settled in the depopulated reach between the two cataracts. These Sudanis are much pleasanter fellows than the Egyptians to work with, though they are far less skilful and have the disadvantage that when under the influence of their beloved " merissa," or native beer, they are rather apt to get out of hand. They are a cheery, open set who admit of a more personal touch than the fellahîn can suffer or contrive, and they have a sense of loyalty and of attachment which makes them much more attractive than the Egyptian, whose horizon is limited to piastres.

At Shablûl we had a very original negro foreman, by name Isgullah. MacIver had given him a little French chiming clock which played the Marseillaise, and Isgullah had so successfully tampered with the works as to induce it to play its tune at the rate of about one note a minute: he used to keep the precious timepiece beside him on the work, wrapped in a red silk handkerchief to protect it from the dust, and each solitary note, as the interminable tune droned out, was echoed by an appreciative grunt from the owner. One day he came to me with his black face all swollen from toothache, and still grinning one-sidedly, begged me to remove the offending ivory. I hastened to refuse, explaining that I had no proper instruments for the operation, whereupon he went off, only to reappear waving a large pair of carpenter's pliers, and begged me to start in at once. I was not going to do anything of the sort, but looked at the tooth and, seeing that it was quite sound, decided that the trouble was probably neuralgia. So I mixed a dose of iodide of potassium and told him to drink it. Isgullah was very contemptuous of the idea.

"What good can that do?" he asked. "It will only go into my stomach, which is all right; but the pain is in the tooth." Still I insisted that he should drink it, and he complied grumblingly. The next morning I saw him at work with his usual cheerful grin, so asked him how he was, and was told that he was well again.

"But, Isgullah, that can't be," I urged; "you said yourself that the medicine could not do any good."

The old nigger looked serious. "It was a very fine medicine," he said, "and did wonderful things. In the night I swallowed my tooth, and it went down into that medicine, and when I woke up it was back in my mouth again quite cured!"

Poor old Isgullah! my drugs were not always to prove so efficacious. After a feast whereat he had indulged too freely in the rare luxury of meat he got violent stomach-ache, and nothing would persuade him that he was not going to die. He took medicines obediently enough, but they could not overcome his conviction, and he just lay under a tree and wasted away. I sent him off to his own village, but he died as he had said he would.

Another old negro workman was equally childlike in his simplicity. Asrag el Arab had, as a boy of thirteen, been servant to a British officer when Korosko was our advance-post against the Mahdi, and he was never tired of extolling his old master's virtues: "But he was mad, very mad," he would add sorrowfully; "it was a pity that so good a man should be mad." I asked him what made him suppose that the officer was insane. "Well," he answered, "he used to shout for me, and I would say, 'Naam!' ('Here am I!'), but he would tell me, 'You must not say "Naam," you must say "Righto!"': was not that madness? Moreover, he would never call me by my proper name. I would say, 'My name is Asrag,' but still he would always call me"—and the old man paused for a deep breath and shouted at the top of his voice—"'Sambò!' I am very sorry that he should have been mad."

His distress was so real that I determined to comfort him. "He was not mad at all," I said, "but you did not understand. *Asrag* means 'black,' and the English for black is Sambo. There was once a very famous Englishman of that name, and we have a book all about him called the 'Book of little Sambò el Asrag'; and so your officer liked to call you after that great Englishman."

He thought it over and seemed satisfied. That night, before going to bed, I walked out into the desert for a breath of air, and there I saw Asrag. The old man was strutting up and down in the moonlight, and each time as he turned on his beat he slapped his bare chest and exclaimed in a voice of pride, "Ana Sambò" ("I am Sambo")—and the name was shouted aloud as his old master had shouted to summon the little house-boy.

Asrag's confidence in the English was indeed touching. He came to the house one day carrying a child about ten years old and said the boy was very ill, could not eat or drink anything, and would I cure him? The boy was apparently in the last stage of diphtheria, his throat almost wholly blocked up, and I felt pretty sure that nothing short of tracheotomy would save him; but as I had no intention of trying that, and knew it was quite useless to explain to Asrag the real nature of the case, I simply told him that I was sorry but could do nothing; the child ought to see a doctor.

"But you cure us all right," he urged; "why won't you do something for the boy?"

"Because you are grown-up men," I answered; "but this is a child and needs a children's doctor, who is quite a different sort."

The argument struck him and he weighed it awhile; then, "But you are an Englishman," said he.

"Well, what of that?"

"If an Englishman takes mud from the Nile and makes pills of it and gives to us, saying, 'Eat this and be well,' by the will of God we are well."

But the child died, and I fear old Asrag always believed that I could have saved it had I wished.

．　　．　　．　　．　　．　　．

Northern Nubia, the Dodekaschoinos of Greek and Roman Egypt, contains a fair number of temples, from Philæ dreaming on its lake-island to Kalabsheh where the grim rocks close in on the Nile and form the famous Gates which bounded the Empire. Guide-books deal at length with this region, and visitors come obediently to inspect the ruins whereof they read. But Southern Nubia, where all my work was done, is still for most people an unfamiliar land. Even the tourists who pass through on the river-steamers see but little of it; they land at Abu Simbel, they climb the rocks of Kasr Ibrim or of

Korosko; but apart from that they do no more than watch idly from the deck the long panorama of river and desert with the strip of green that separates the two. Sometimes, as at Tomas, Anibeh, and Argin, the sandstone hills fall back and leave room for cultivation on a larger scale, and the palm-groves and fields of durra may be as much as half a mile in width, but more often it is but a ribbon of green that edges the river, a shelving bank of lentils topped by a fringe of blue-grey castor-oil plants or yellow-tasselled acacia, in all not twenty yards across; and sometimes even this fails, and rock or sand runs down, unrelieved by any living growth, to the hurried waters of the Nile. It is a barren place—too barren, one would suppose, ever to have supported more than the few straggling villages which to-day are strung along the skirts of the desert—too barren, certainly, to have played a part in history or to have been fought for by great nations. Yet this inhospitable land has had its full share of the clash of civilizations and of war. Narrow as it is, a country of rock and river, it has always been the highway between the fertile valley of Egypt and the fabled South. He who would from Egypt control the Sudan must hold Nubia, and therefore from the time of the early Pharaohs to our own these rocks have echoed to the tramp of armies, the river has borne warships sailing southwards and merchant-vessels drifting north, and in the few fertile reaches forts and walled towns have secured the desert road.

And all these things have left their mark. True,

it is not a land of great monuments, and, with the splendid exception of Abu Simbel, can put forward nothing to rival the vast ruins of Egypt; the tourist southward-bound is perhaps well advised to be content with the view from his steamer's deck. Yet if one be not pressed for time nor sated with antiquities, there is much even here eloquent of the past, and sometimes of more modern happenings no less dramatic.

When I was digging at Karanog town, four miles or so north of Anibeh, we noticed running inland from the river along the southern edge of the ruins what at first glance seemed the top of a broad wall buried in the sand. I moved a few stones and found clean sand below—it was no wall, but a causeway: I followed it up over a low rise and across a narrow dip; it climbed a second rise, and there before me on the level ground lay a British camp! There was the stone zariba, foursquare and complete, with its gates and broad main street: rings of big boulders, arranged in ordered lines, showed where the tent-ropes had been made fast, and in the circles where the tents had stood the gravel was swept smooth and clean; even the broken medicine-bottles lay there to mark the site of the hospital. The camp might have been deserted but yesterday, yet in fact these stones are a monument of the Mahdist War—a monument which in that lifeless, changeless desert will last as long as all the books written about the Nile Campaign. Go to the hills above Korosko, and in the gravel of the upper plateau you will see the ruts of the wheels of transport-wagons and of guns where Hicks Pasha and his ill-starred army set out to cross the desert: the ruts are still clear and sharp, though Hicks Pasha and all his men have been dead these thirty years.

These are records of yesterday, as it were, alone, but there are other spots in Nubia which sum up in themselves the whole long history of the land. The tourist who climbs up the bluff whereon, three hundred feet sheer above the Nile, are the clustered ruins of Kasr Ibrim, is generally more interested in the wide view along the river valley or in the sunset which paints the desert saffron and purple than in the tumble-down houses of dry rubble all around him; but this rock-castle has seen many events in its time. Look straight across the river where, just above Anibeh village, the level rays of the sun throw into relief certain long mounds enclosing a broken space all hillocks and hollows; these are the ruins of Ma'am, Ma'am which was a walled town before Rameses the First was born. On the gravel plateau above is the cemetery of its people, a few of the pyramid-chapels of crude brick still standing there, ruined now, and with the frescoes peeling from their walls, to show what a New Kingdom grave was like; some of the chief men lay in rock-hewn tombs under your feet, and the doors of the rifled chambers look out from the cliff's face towards the forgotten city where they lived. It may well be that the rocky summit itself was crowned by a temple of the Ramessids: I have found a few inscribed blocks from such among the castle ruins, and though it is quite possible that these were brought over from the town site on the western bank to be re-used in a building of a later age, yet it seems hardly likely that the Egyptians would have overlooked the advantages of this bold, rocky bluff, whose sanctity is in a measure guaranteed by the tomb-shafts driven into its face. But however this may be, the standing remains upon the height belong to another age and another civilization than does the town of Ma'am.

At the north end of the fortified enclosure, where the rock plateau shrinks to a narrow spit overlooking the river, there stands, still fairly well preserved, a small temple of finely-cut ashlar, Egyptian indeed in general style, but singularly severe and unadorned; only the uræus over the doorway relieves the simplicity of the massive stonework. This is a Meroïtic shrine.

When the sun of the greater Ramessids went down in anarchy and weakness, in the far South there rose to independence an Æthiopian power whose swarthy kings in the XXVth Dynasty overran and for a time ruled Egypt as Pharaohs. Driven out thence by the invading arms of Persia, they set themselves to develop their own land of the Sudan. Certain Egyptian priests who took asylum with them from Persian iconoclasts for a while eclipsed the monarchy and had to be put down with a strong hand; but though they were beaten in their bid for temporal power, they set their mark upon the land of their adoption, and went far to complete the Egyptianizing process which the rule of earlier Pharaohs over the South and the South's conquest of Egypt had begun. The worship of Isis was firmly grafted on to whatever barbarous beliefs had held sway at Meroë, Egyptian writing was adapted to the uses of the native tongue, and Egyptian art was encouraged by the lords of the Sudan; the Meroïtic Empire was not Egyptian, but it had absorbed enough of Egyptian culture to raise it far above what could have been expected of a hybrid negro race ruled by an aristocracy of Semitic immigrants. Thus it was that, when Egypt fell under Greek rule, the heirs of Alexander who wore the crown of Upper and Lower Egypt found their southern neighbours willing, upon the whole, to enter into friendly relations with them, and able to imbibe something at least of their new civilization. The Gates of Kalabsheh, where the narrowing river runs swift and strong between walls of rocks, formed the boundary between the two kingdoms, for the Meroïtic sovereigns had taken advantage of the weakness of the Saïte Pharaohs to push up through the "Belly of Stones," which is the Second Cataract, and to establish themselves in Southern Nubia, building their forts wherever a wider stretch of fertile soil gave such chance of livelihood as a desert folk might covet; but they made no effort to come farther north, nor had the Ptolemies much interest in the land already occupied now that it was no longer the high road to any possessions southwards. Only trade-ships and peaceful caravans passed the frontier, bringing Greek goods and Greek ideas to the Meroïtic folk, who copied or freely adapted these, and from the mixture of Central Africa, Egypt, and Greece evolved an art which was not any of these, but was unique of its kind.

It was about this time that the temple of Kasr Ibrim was built and a wall thrown up around the rock plateau: strong by nature and strongly fortified, Primis was the main bulwark of the northern colony of Meroë. Nor was it very long before such defences were required. Egypt fell before Rome. Cleopatra, last of the Ptolemies, was minded when all seemed lost to find asylum with her Meroïtic friends, but events moved too quickly for her; she died by her own hand, and her sons, whom she had sent on south before her, were murdered by a faithless tutor anxious to curry favour with Octavius. But the Candace who then ruled in the Sudan was not inclined to welcome the Romans as she had favoured the Greeks, and her armies passed through the Kalabsheh Gates to snatch something of the spoil from the victor's hands. Border troubles vexed the new Roman province, and even the city of Aswân and the holy island of Elephantiné were taken and put to the sack, and the bronze bust of the Emperor Augustus carried off as a trophy to Meroë.[1]

---

[1] And at Meroë it remained till the twentieth century. When brought to light by the excavator's spade it journeyed afresh, to find a final resting-place in the capital of another Empire, this time on Thames' bank.

To avenge this insult the legate Petronius Gallus invaded Nubia, and from the towers of Primis the Æthiopians could see the legions in long line advancing up the western bank and deploying for the battle there, where the main forces of Queen Candace were drawn up to dispute the road; and from those towers they watched too the rout of their people and the massacre of the fugitives. Then crossing the river, Petronius seized the city. The strength of its position appealed to the military instincts of the legate, who was anxious to add a new province to the Empire; so, while he pushed southwards into Dongola, and at Napata (now Gebel Barkal) reduced the African queen to terms, a force left behind at Kasr Ibrim was busy re-fortifying the place and transforming it into a Roman outpost. He must have been no little disgusted when two months later he received peremptory orders from Augustus to evacuate the conquered territory and to retire behind the old frontier of Kalabsheh. He dismantled the defences he had laboriously thrown up, and withdrew.

Years passed, and a new factor entered into the problem. Probably about the close of the first century A.D. the Blemmyes, an offshoot of the Meroïtic Empire, whose language and civilization they shared, began to filter in to the marshes laid waste by the Roman legions and to establish themselves on the deserted sites. At an early stage they set to work to repair the breaches in the walls of Kasr Ibrim, and to put it again in a state of defence. No sooner were they settled down and their strongholds built—at Karanog, at Faras, Tomas, and elsewhere—than they started to raid the Roman province of Egypt, and endless trouble did they cause to its rulers. Even Diocletian, though he claims to have conquered them, did not succeed in stamping out the pest; on the contrary, he withdrew the Roman frontier from Kalabsheh to Aswân, bringing in the Nubians or Nobatai to occupy the territory thus relinquished and to form a buffer state, while with the Blemmyes he made such terms as confirmed their religious privileges at Philæ, secured their political independence, and gave them an annual subsidy to boot. But the raiding continued as before.

Kasr Ibrim played no part in these happenings, for the fighting was all to the north, sometimes indeed far into Egypt, where the marauding bands pushed up to Luxor and beyond. The castle enjoyed a time of peace, a village grew up on the opposite bank close to the great cemetery, and for four hundred years the walls were not called upon to resist an enemy. Then in A.D. 540 the end came. The Empire was now Christian, and not only were the Blemmyes persistent border-thieves, but they were too the last of the Isis-worshippers, and the terms whereby Diocletian had guaranteed their religious rights at Philæ were intolerable to a Christian emperor. In alliance, therefore, with the Nubian king Silko, an opportune convert, Justinian declared war on the stubborn pagans: the combined forces in two campaigns stormed Kasr Ibrim and exterminated its defenders. The Blemmyes now disappear from history.[1]

Under the tutelage of Byzantium the Nubians settled down in the conquered territory, and Kasr Ibrim became a Christian city. The old temple was not destroyed, but in the centre of the town there rose a fine church whose ashlar walls and columns, with decorated capitals, are still conspicuous amongst the ruins; the Christian dead were buried on the low ground beneath the castle rock, where the crowded brick tomb-chapels stand to-day.

Very soon after, the new faith arose which was in its turn to supplant Christianity in North Africa and the Near East; but though Egypt fell before the Moslem arms, and in A.D. 641 the Arabs raided upstream as far as Dongola, yet this was only a raid; the wave retreated to the old Roman frontier, and the walled forts of the Nubians long sufficed to keep out the Crescent from their barren reaches. It was not till the twelfth century that Shems ed Doulah, brother of Saladin, advancing southwards, laid waste the many churches of Christian Nubia. Then once more Kasr Ibrim was taken by assault. The church became a mosque, and the later tomb-chapels at the foot of the rock are those of the True Believers who

[1] It would be tempting, though it would be unwarranted by any evidence, to see them again in the pagan tribes which about A.D. 850 attacked Upper Egypt, withheld the tribute from the gold-mines, and spread terror over the land. They were put down at the cost of much bloodshed, and their leader, one Ali Baba, was admitted to terms and carried off to Samarra on the Tigris. His tribe still held to their creed though serving under the Moslems, and the Caliph's court was scandalized to find Ali Baba carrying about with him the stone idol of his worship.

now held the land. But now there was no enemy to be kept out, and the useless defences fell into disrepair; the population of the town dwindled as men, living without fear, moved down from the cliff-top to low-lying villages closer to their fields; it would seem that by the beginning of the nineteenth century Kasr Ibrim was wellnigh if not quite deserted.

But the old fort was to know one more adventure. In 1811 the ruler of Egypt, Mohammed Ali, finding that his Mameluk bodyguard was becoming too strong for its master, determined to rid himself of the danger, and gave orders for a general massacre. Most of them fell victims to his treachery, but some of these Bosnian troops escaped, and, fighting their way southwards, sought asylum in Nubia; seeing Kasr Ibrim on its sheer cliff above the Nile, they seized on that, and for a while the old Blemmyan fort became a Bosnian city of refuge. But the Khedive's troops were upon the track of the fugitives; there was a last assault, the Mameluks were wiped out, and the town was finally ruined and left to its decay.

No inscriptions commemorate at Kasr Ibrim the many changes it has known, but all or nearly all have left their mark upon its walls. Look at the old temple of Candace's time, and then if you clamber round the town walls you will see here a few courses, there a buttress wellnigh complete, where the stones dressed in the same fashion as those of the temple show that here you have the defences which Petronius stormed after routing the field army of the one-eyed queen. Look again, and you will see, hard against this Meroïtic masonry, work of another sort—the squared stones are large but differently dressed, or most of them are, for here and there a Meroïtic block is built in amongst them—good solid walling, but, as you follow it round, breached in many places to its foundations, and seeming wantonly destroyed. Here, and it needs no imagination to see it, Petronius threw down the ramparts which he had himself not fully built, Roman walls which he could not leave whole to shelter the enemies of Rome. There, again, these breaches are filled with more slipshod work of smaller rubble less truly laid, the hurried labour of the Blemmyes who, new-come to the land, made all haste to repair the old defences. And so it is throughout: fresh breaches and fresh patchings mark the vicissitudes of a town which so often changed its masters, and fresh courses were added above as the ground-level rose. The rubbish of centuries, flung outside the gate to free the narrow confines of the plateau, was heaped up there until the gate itself was choked, and the walls must needs be raised and a new gateway built whose threshold was the carved lintel of the older door. The simple shrine, the church, and these patched and crumbling ramparts, which seem so small a thing to eyes sated with the temples and pyramids of Egypt, are yet a record of dead peoples and forgotten fights which it were surely worth while to stop and read before the sunset calls all one's thoughts to the eternal wonder of sky and desert.

Faras, farther up the river, has an even longer record than Kasr Ibrim can boast, reaching back before the dawn of history and continuing to our own time. The Nile here has changed its course, and the old river ran half a mile or more west of the present stream. It was on the west bank of this dried-up bed that we discovered in 1911 a small cemetery of the Ist Egyptian Dynasty (the civilization of Nubia and of Middle Egypt was all one five thousand years ago), and on the gravel of the desert's edge were clear to see the traces of a village of those far-off days. A few lines of rough stones showed where huts had stood, and within these the hearths were still marked by smoke-blackened stones and ash; fragments of pottery lay all about, rubbers and mortars of stone, pieces of worked bone and ostrich-shell, flint implements and masses of flint chips struck off when the implements were in the making. The tombs of course yielded far better "finds"—polished celts, slate palettes, unbroken vases, and all the furniture of a burial such as one finds in Egypt; but somehow the deserted village site, scanty as were its remains, spoke more vividly of the life lived so long ago. Here these people lit their fires and plied their simple crafts; their huts, mere piled stones roofed in with tent-cloth, maybe, or with reeds and boughs, were the same as one sees used nowadays in the barren valleys of Sinai. I remember an old Bedouin whom I found brewing his morning drink of tamarisk tea on just such a hearth, in just such a rude shelter, one cold spring morning in the tangled

FARAS: DIGGING UP MEROITIC GRAVES.

In the foreground are the remains of a Coptic church, in the left middle distance the ruins of Akhenaton's Temple. Behind the tent stretches a row of tamarisk sand-hills.

wilderness east of Kadesh. The very simplicity of their life makes it dateless, and bridges the gulf of its five thousand years; in their graves these ancient folk strove to achieve perpetuity, but, all unwitting, they left a more lively record in the open desert.

The history of Faras throughout the Middle Kingdom and the New Empire, under Meroïtic and under Christian rule, has been recorded elsewhere; at all those times, and not least during the last, it was a flourishing city, and in melancholy contrast to that prosperous age are the huts of the modern village and the narrowing fields on which year by year the sand-dunes steadily encroach.

These dunes are one of the wonders of the place. Look at them, and you would say that they were but steep hills of drift-sand covered with low-growing scrub, long ridges and cone-shaped mounds that threaten from the west the fields of durra and lucerne. The truth is the reverse of the appearance: it is not the growth that veils the sand, but the sand that shrouds the living tree. The husbandman of an earlier day, Meroïtic or Christian, planted tamarisk hedges to protect his fields; the wind-borne sand caught in the thick spiny growth and formed mounds against the bushes, but these pushed their branches through the drift and still formed a barrier. More sand blew on, the mounds grew higher, and still the bushes struggled to keep their heads clear, until now they are trees sixty or a hundred feet high, the tips of whose branches only push out from the sides and tops of the dunes, while their trunks go down through the centre to the solid ground beneath. Many are dead now, and the winds, finding the sand bared of the greenery which sheltered it, undo their old work and carry it forwards over the fields where a later and less provident folk have devised no barrier against the yellow tide. I have seen elsewhere, at Khalassa for instance, in the Sinai desert below Beersheba, just such long lines of tamarisk, Byzantine hedge-rows, showing through the sand-drifts, but nowhere else have I seen them as at Faras, towering aloft in banks up which it is hard to scramble, one hundred feet above the plain.

There is at Faras one more monument of history, and that of a later date. When in 1889 Wad Nejumi started against his will on the last hopeless venture to conquer Egypt for the Khalifa, an English force from Halfa marched with him, keeping ever between him and the river. The thirsty multitude—for their women and children came with the fighting men to settle down in Egypt—pressed along the desert edge, and over against Faras followed the valley that is the old bed of the Nile; and from the monastery mound of Faras and from the river the English guns shelled them as they passed. If to-day you climb the sand-hills of the buried tamarisk groves and look down on the long trough which separates them from the gravel desert, it looks as if a school paper-chase had passed that way. But they are bones that whiten the valley bottom, bones of men and horses and camels, tatters of cloth and tags of leather, the debris of an army

FARAS: THE COPTIC MONASTERY ON THE HILL.

EGYPT

beaten or ever it was crushed at Toski. Thus Faras, starting at the beginning of things with the ruins of its stone-age village, can show, but a hundred yards or so therefrom, relics of the last war the Nile Valley has known, and of the last invasion which threatened Egypt from the South.

Whether the changes of history have left their mark upon the people as they have upon the buildings of Nubia it is difficult to say; these folk are not given to talking about themselves to foreigners, and, question as one may, it is hard to elicit from them anything of interest. But a chance encounter once showed us that there is in some things a continuity of tradition which goes back to early times.

Mr. and Mrs. Griffith and myself had gone out one day from Faras to picnic in the desert where from the gravel plateau there rises an isolated hill whose semi-sacred character made us suppose that an older sanctity might have been retained into the Moslem age. It was said that a Mohammedan saint was buried here, but as he had no name other than "the Sheikh el Gebel" (the Hill or Desert Sheikh), his authenticity was not above suspicion. In fact, the so-called grave proved to be but a rough stone enclosure at the hill's foot, a mere zariba, nearly circular, with an opening facing towards the hill, the whole bearing no resemblance to a Moslem tomb. But in the hill itself a cave with Christian *graffiti* on its walls showed that before the Mohammedan faith prevailed an earlier hermit had settled here and hallowed the spot, while a few Egyptian hieroglyphs on the rocks pointed to the possibility that even he had been attracted hither by religious associations older still.

We had finished our search and were at lunch when across the desert a little procession was to be seen coming towards us. At its head was a man driving a donkey laden with firewood, behind him walked a young man bearing a kid across his shoulders, then an old bearded fellow who carried a long knife, and behind him women with a cooking-pot, bags of flour, and bunches of herbs. It was another picnic party, but in this case a religious one, come out to do sacrifice. The young man who carried the goat was a Berberine of Faras who had just completed four years' domestic service in Cairo; before he left home his father had vowed to sacrifice on his son's return a kid to the Sheikh el Gebel, and now the young man had come back to get married and the vow was to be performed.

In a corner by the entrance to the Sheikh's zariba, where the blackened stones showed that the ceremony was no unwonted thing, a fire was kindled and the cauldron was set on it; the kid's throat was cut, it was skinned and cleaned, and set to boil "with bitter herbs" in the pot. While it was cooking, the men of the party went in turn into the enclosure and prayed, and the women kneaded flour and baked their flat unleavened loaves on hot stones pulled out from the fireplace. Then all set to and ate, and afterwards collected the fragments of bread and meat, which might neither be thrown away nor kept till the morrow, but must be given to the poor of the village. It was a curiously old-world scene, and quite un-Mohammedan; the manner of the sacrifice was Semitic, brought from the Eastern desert where things were done just so in days when Abraham shifted his camp there with the changing seasons, and the place of it was a "holy mount" whose sanctity was derived from an alien faith, and a saint long since forgotten. Just as at Karanog I heard dim legends of an old king "Kara" who dwelt in the ruined castle and thence levied toll on the trade-boats passing up and down the river, so it may well be that the modern Berberine preserves many traditions which might throw light upon the history of this troubled borderland.

I have tried to show how, as in the case of Kasr Ibrim, a place not very attractive at first sight may by the results of archæological work be made interesting, and I have perhaps been too long in the attempt; but at any rate I have dealt with results, which are history, and not with archæological detail. For the details of archæology are but raw material, and one should not try to present the records of an expedition in popular form; apart from the artistic merit of particular objects, it is only the historical results at which the general public should be asked to look. So I have little to say about our actual work in Egypt, seeing that this is neither a scientific record nor a history, and as for the methods of digging there, they have been described too often to stand repetition. Indeed, one excavator's experience in Egypt is very much like every other's, apart from his actual finds: he has his work and his workmen, both demanding care and study, but he meets with no adventure worthy of the name, and if things go wrong he has confident recourse to the law. To tell the truth, Egypt is dull. Its archæology as such is interesting, but the country is too peaceful and civilized to allow of much incident, and the joyous occurrences of Carchemish would be impossible in the smooth tenor of Egyptian life.

Nor is the Egyptian fellah whom for the most part one employs a very sympathetic person. He is a hard worker, and with experience becomes very skilful when called upon for delicate work; he is shrewd enough to have a very fair idea of the value of his finds and of their relative date, but he has remarkably little real interest in his work and less in you; with him it is a question of wages and baksheesh and no more.

The system of baksheesh, *i.e.* of giving rewards for objects found, is very generally adopted in Egypt, and is vehemently opposed by those excavators who do not practise it; for my own part I have found it the best, not in Egypt only but anywhere where digging is to be done. It is perfectly true that if you employ a man to dig up antiquities for you and pay him a fair regular wage, he has no claim whatsoever upon what he finds; legally the thing is on the same footing as diamond-mining. But the legal view leaves out of account the psychological element; the mere fact of finding what was hidden in the earth does give a sense of possession, of personal good luck, and with that feeling you must reckon. In Egypt, where the workman acknowledges no real loyalty to his employer, and has no scruples about stealing what he has found, the rule has grown up of paying him as a reward the sum that a travelling dealer would be likely to offer for the antiquity in question; consequently the reward is generally in inverse proportion to the bulk of the object: for a fine scarab, easily concealed and commanding a ready market, you have to pay good market value, while for a big stone that could not be stolen you may give a nominal sum. In North Syria, where the workman's sense of honour does away with all risk of theft, the criterion is not the same; you pay more by the real importance of the find, or use the system to give encouragement and to promote care, but baksheesh remains a necessary thing, because it appeals to the sporting element in the Arab. I have had hundreds of men, earning from twelve to twenty piastres a day on the Bagdad Railway, clamouring to be taken on by us as diggers at eight or nine piastres, and while there were other reasons at work, yet not the least was the prospect of a gamble—the chance that one morning's work may bring in a sovereign, even though the rest of the season mean nothing more than the regulation wage. Moreover, the system ensures good work. To cut down a man's earnings is an invidious thing, and not understood of the native, but he quite sees the justice of your not paying him extra for what he has broken by his clumsiness, and in a very little while will learn to take as much pride in his skill as pleasure in the reward it wins him.

It is just the same with British workmen. They quite realize that you are making no material profit out of the digging, so have not that sense of being exploited for your advantage which often sets them against their employer; but your pleasure in a "find" is naturally greater than theirs. Balance things by a small baksheesh, and they become your partners in the game. Then if the historical interest of objects fails to touch their imagination, get local patriotism into play, and you will have a gang keen on the work for its own sake. I remember well that when we found our first piece of Roman sculpture at Corbridge-on-Tyne, a lion from a fountain, the first question raised by the workmen was whether this were not a finer thing than the famous horseman relief on a tombstone in Hexham Abbey, and the assurance that Corbridge had outdone the rival town gave a satisfaction far more lasting than the extra cash.

But with the Egyptian the baksheesh is always an end in itself, and the only end, so that scanty finds mean a discontented and a troublesome gang. At Halfa one of our workmen, a good digger and as a rule a lucky one, grew so melancholy because his baksheesh account did not come up to his hopes that he developed homicidal mania and beheaded his wife and daughter. Of course, that was an extreme case, and even the worst of seasons does not fill one's camp with armed lunatics; but the fact remains that the fellah works with you for what he can get, and has no idea above money; he takes no interest in you, and it is therefore not easy to take much in him, or indeed to know much about him. The archæologist comes more closely into touch with his workmen than do most European employers, but none the less he remains for them an alien: for a higher wage they will take service elsewhere without regret; they will cheat him if it be to their advantage, and will steal outright from him if they think his baksheesh niggardly and the risk of detection not too great.

The fact is that the Egyptian does not like the Englishman or the English Government; it is partly a religious question, for Mohammedanism is more intolerant in Egypt than almost anywhere else, and partly political. The fellah, who more than any other class has benefited by our rule, is aware that our presence is on the whole to his interest, but its tangible advantages must be kept very clearly before his eyes if they are to outbalance its defects, for his historical memory is short and the old regime too much a thing of the past to suffice as a standing contrast. I have known a peasant, who had heard that some money he had sent home by post was overdue, complain bitterly that he could see no use in having a Government at all if a man could not send money about in safety; thirty years before he would not have dared to let the Government know that he had any money, but that change in the general condition of things never struck him. Granted that we are in Egypt to stay, what the fellah does want, to reconcile him to our rule, is more British inspectors in the provinces. As it is, the number of these has been seriously diminished, and while our officials overcrowd the Government bureaux in Cairo and have often not enough business to keep them employed throughout a three hours' working day, the villager is left to the mercies of his own countrymen, with the result that petty corruption is as general and as oppressive as it was in 1880. I have overheard an Egyptian fellah talking with a Sudan native and contrasting the conditions of their lives; each side found the other's description almost incomprehensible. The Egyptian talked of the bribing of judges that must accompany a lawsuit, and the Sudani declared such a thing impossible—until it was explained that one spoke of native judges and the other of English. An epidemic in a border village brought up the question of sanitary inspectors and medical officers, and here again the Egyptians were full of stories of corruption. These are the things that touch the peasant most closely, and it is not altogether surprising that he should be blinded by them to the broader issues of good *versus* bad government, and fail to appreciate the benefits that seem so obvious to the Englishman.

Perhaps the most annoying characteristic of the Egyptian is his absolute disregard of truth. Personally I do not think that he is the wilful liar that he seems, but rather that he has not the same conception of truth as ourselves, and does not distinguish as we do between subjective and objective reality. An idea, even one newly born, may appeal to him as true though it flatly contradict facts with which he is familiar; after all, they are both ideas in his head, and he gives the preference to that which most appeals to his taste or answers best to the needs of the moment.

One day MacIver and I were copying some inscriptions cut on a rock that stands out from the Nile bank just below the Nubian village of Tomas, when a villager who had been watching us for a while in silence asked what we were doing. We said, "Looking at the inscriptions." He asked whether we were interested in such things, and when we said we were, inquired further whether we had seen the "temple" at the farther end of the village. As we did not believe that such a thing existed, we said "No," rather curtly, and asked him what he meant. In reply, the fellow gave us a very fair description of a New Empire rock-tomb. There was, he said, cut in a rock-face behind the village a doorway having writing above it; on either side was a statue, but these were so damaged that he did not know what they were meant to be. Inside was a small room, whose walls were covered with figures and writing—painted in colours, but at the same time cut in the stone—and behind this was a smaller room not decorated at all, but with a hole in the floor. He knew the place well, in fact everybody knew it, because it was a favourite playground for the village children. Three other villagers had strolled up and overheard the latter part of the story, and the narrator appealed to them for confirmation. Two of the new-comers agreed with all that was said, and added a few details; the third said he had never seen the thing himself, but knew of it from hearsay. Rather puzzled, for such a rock-tomb was unknown in the district, we cross-questioned the men, but could not shake their statements; at last they seemed hurt at our disbelief, and volunteered to show us the place. We told the first informant that we would go with him, and if satisfied would give baksheesh; otherwise he would get a kicking for deceiving us. He agreed readily enough, and we all moved off towards the lower end of the village. On the way MacIver pointed to some rude rock-drawings such as are common in Nubia, and date from all periods between the prehistoric and the present day, and asked whether that were the sort of thing we were to expect; the men grew quite indignant at the suggestion, and repeated their detailed account of the tomb. We walked for three-quarters of an hour, and just as we were growing impatient our guide pointed to a rock-face wherein, he said, the cave was cut. The rock-face stood not more than four feet high, too low to allow for a door—and of a door there was not the remotest sign.

"Here is the place," said the three men.

"Where is the tomb?" said we.

The chief guide looked puzzled. "It certainly *was* here," he said; "perhaps the sand has covered it up," and going down on his knees he began to scoop away the drift-sand at the foot of the rock—only to find that a fresh rock-shelf ran out but a few inches below the surface. The story was palpably absurd. But those villagers insisted still that the tomb had always been there, that they had played in it as boys, and that this was the very spot; their only explanation for its non-appearance was that some jinn, to cheat them of their reward, had before our arrival carried the cave bodily away!

I do not believe that the thing was a practical joke. The men had a long tramp and an unpleasantly violent cursing at the end of it; nor is the Egyptian fellah given to such jests. It seems to me a case of auto-suggestion; the first man, seeing our interest in what looked to him poor scratches in the cliff, thought how splendid it would be if he could show us such a decorated "temple" as he had heard tell of in other parts—and at once the temple was to him a reality, and the reward for its discovery as good as in his pocket. The other men adopted the idea with the same readiness, and it became as truly a part of their experience as were their own houses in the village. Every archæologist in Egypt has been told of the great temples in the desert behind Abu Simbel; how two days' or three days' journey westward from the Nile you may find buildings vaster and more glorious than the rock-cut shrines of Rameses themselves. Some natives have seen them, others go on hearsay only, but many are prepared to guide you to this undiscovered marvel. These tales are lies, but it is no use to call those that tell them liars, for they are thoroughly persuaded of their truth.

There is an amusing story which shows how readily the fellah will believe what is to his advantage, even when there are no Europeans to be fooled. In Kuft there is a shrine of some local holy man, a little shrine served by a local mullah, whereto pilgrims were wont to come with offerings from the neighbouring villages. As time went on the saint's merits began to be forgotten, the pilgrims grew fewer, and the tale of offerings diminished sadly.

One Friday the mullah announced to his congregation that he had three times running dreamed a wonderful dream:

"I stood," he said, "on the river bank, and there came floating down the stream two great rocks, greater than a man could lift, and one drifted on down below the village and went out of sight, but one came to the shore hard by where I stood. And as I watched, the rock moved slowly up the steep bank where Hassan Ahmed's lentils are, and then rolled on through Ibrahim Suliman's durra patch, up to the houses and along the village street to this shrine, and it entered the door and came to rest below the mimbar from which I speak to you to-day. And I dreamed that from that day the fame of this shrine grew great again, and pilgrims flocked in from all around, and their offerings were as rich as they were in years gone by."

The sermon gave rise to a good deal of discussion, which was changed to awe and wonder when two mornings later the report came in that a great stone was in fact lying at the water's edge below the village; all flocked out to see the portent, and to discuss its connection with the mullah's dream. The next day Hassan Ahmed was loudly bewailing the damage done to his lentils, but the stone was lying now upon the top of the steep river bank. On the following day the villagers came out from the houses wherein they had carefully barred themselves all night for fear of such supernatural powers as were abroad, to find Ibrahim Suliman's durra crop all crushed and trampled and the great stone lying in the middle of the village street. Here was' miracle clear and beyond cavil, and no one was surprised when the next morning saw the stone safely ensconced in the little shrine. The news was published far and wide, the sanctity of the saint was vindicated, and the mullah reaped a handsome profit. Not a man but believed that spiritual agencies had been at work. Even the somewhat free-thinking villager who told the story was convinced of its truth, and in proof thereof pointed to the fact that the stone was indeed too heavy for any man to lift; only when asked whether one man, given plenty of time, could have *rolled* it up the bank and onward did he burst into laughter, and admit that no one had ever thought of that!

This power of suggestion is not confined to the fellahîn. In the midsummer of 1915, nearly six months after Jemal Pasha's army had been driven back from the Canal, an educated Egyptian, high in the Civil Service, was firmly convinced that the Turks were and had been all along in undisputed possession of Port Said, Ismailia, and Suez; no amount of argument could shake his belief, and it required a personally-conducted tour to the Canal zone to persuade him that the British were still masters there. A year later the same conviction was held by quite a number of upper-class Egyptians, and though again a visit to the Canal silenced them for the moment, it is likely enough that within a week or so the old belief had effaced such impression as mere facts had made upon their minds.

For when an Egyptian has once got an idea into his head it is very hard to disabuse him of it. When I first went to Jerablus I took with me for my photographic work two Egyptian boys; one had been trained by Dr. Reisner and the other by Griffith and myself, and they were both of them experienced and, so far as my requirements went, capable photographers. One day I went into the newly-installed dark-room and found the two boys plunged in stubborn despair over the china developing-dishes.

"What are these things for?" they asked.

I told them, and they groaned. "Developing-dishes are made of metal," they said; "it is impossible to develop photographs in these things."

No amount of argument could move them, and they had to be driven into making the experiment by threats of being sent straight back to Egypt if they didn't. The photographs came out all right, but to the end of their time nothing would convince those Egyptians that china was not an inferior substitute for enamelled tin and an added difficulty to their trade.

ITALY

A FOREIGNER does not often get the chance of doing field-work in Italy. Italian archæologists look upon the interference of strangers in their country with a jealousy which is natural enough, and is further justified by the splendid work done by themselves. The Government, comparatively poor though it be, spends yearly upon excavations and upon the upkeep of national monuments an amount of money which the British public would grudge in a decade, and for carrying out its excavations there is no lack of capable men. To get permission to dig is therefore no easy matter for an outsider, and, as the law is chary of allowing the export of antiquities, it is equally hard for him to find funds for work which can bring in but small material recompense to those who finance it. For the greater part of my time in Italy, then, I was busied only with such investigations as are open to all, and it was by a stroke of unusually good luck that I was able on one site to carry out regular excavations on a large scale.

Teano, a hill-town hard by the railway line from Rome to Naples, Teanum Sidicinum of the ancient Sabines, was my headquarters, and the actual site

TEANO: THE ROMAN BATHS DURING EXCAVATION.

chosen was that of the city baths, lying some four miles away from the modern town. The building, provincial though it was, had played a part in history, for in the second century B.C. an incident occurred here fraught with dire results. The Roman Consul, while on tour, visited Teanum, and his wife wished to take a bath. It was not a ladies' day, but the bathrooms were cleared and the distinguished dame had them to herself. But she complained that the place was dirty, and her indignant husband laid hands on the local magistrates and had them flogged for their negligence. It was a scandalous abuse of authority against the officers of an allied, not a subject, state, and the riot that followed led to the outbreak of a war between Rome and the Latin races. Though, of course, in the centuries through which they remained in use the baths had been re-modelled and re-adorned, it seemed not unreasonable to hope that some remains of their earlier as well as of their late Imperial stages might be brought to light, but this hope was doomed to disappointment. Indeed, the work, though interesting enough in itself, was not very remunerative, and since all my results—notes, plans, and photographs — were published without acknowledgement by a fellow-scientist,[1] I got but small professional satisfaction out of it; but the conditions of life were delightful, and make Teano one of the pleasantest of memories.

An old friend, Baron Zarone, had lent me a set of rooms in his palazzo, once the stronghold of the

[1] "Teano," by Dottore G Gabrici, in *Notizie degli Scavi*.

mediæval hill-men, and one could not ask for better quarters. The great courtyard opening off the town's main square had been modernized in the eighteenth century with doubtful taste, though the broad staircase of pink and white marble redeemed to some extent the dullness of the rest; but at the back the massive grey walls had suffered little change during the six centuries and more which had weathered and mellowed them. From their foot sloped down a terraced garden, beautiful in neglect, where the straggling rose-bushes of the upper levels made splashes of colour against the glossy leaves of orange-trees and nespolas below, and farther down the silvery olives led the eye on over field and vineyard to the far hills and to Vesuvius' squat cone with its flower of faint and shifting cloud. Teano was indeed an ideal spot for a holiday had one been seeking such. The town with its narrow stair-like streets, its hanging gardens, and its girdle of old walls was picturesque enough to satisfy the soul of any artist. Below lie the ruins of the amphitheatre, vast and sombre, and the whole smiling country-side is dotted with relics of the historic past—broken walls and tombs, Oscan inscriptions on stones built into modern field-walls, and Roman milestones in the hedges. Farther afield there are glorious walks to be made, and one such walk which I took in company with the Director of the British School at Rome was something not to be forgotten. We followed the Roman road which for miles runs across country, paved with polygonal blocks of dark-grey tufa, now polished by the feet of centuries, shaded by great trees and dotted with wayside shrines; then over lonely pastures and uphill till in the afternoon we reached our goal, a high-set fastness of the early Sabines, known nowadays as Queen Joanna's Garden, whose cyclopean walls half-hidden in chestnut scrub were haunted, so a timorous goat-herd warned us, by heaven knows what ghosts of old marauders; then pushing through the thick undergrowth we fell into a leaf-filled torrent-bed and, hidden from one another by a brown whirlwind, we slid, literally slid, nearly two hundred yards downhill till we pulled up breathless with laughter on the lower levels. Through the beech-woods we went on to Fontana Fredda, where, famished after our long day, we washed down our dry bread with the water that spouts from three holes in the rock into a marble basin—ice-cold the water was, and oh! how good! —and so to a little village where we were fain to dine, and instead were all but arrested by a too zealous carabiniere as German spies, and found that we had yet ten miles to tramp through the dark before reaching Teano and our beds.

Another pleasant excursion was to Calvi Risorta, the ancient Cales, where they made in Greek times the bowls of fine black-varnished pottery with ornament in high relief known to archæologists as Calene phialæ. Excavations on the property of a friend of mine, Signor Nobile, had recently proved that Teano also had a peculiar pottery of its own, a black ware with incised and painted flower-designs, and I was curious to see whether further search at Calvi, where little digging had been done, would not throw fresh light on the local fabrics. I could not carry out any excavations, as I had no licence for such, but luck served me well, for in exploring the acropolis I found, laid bare where the soil of the hillside had slipped away, a great heap of pottery fragments, perhaps a refuse pile where discarded temple-offerings were thrown, which yielded quite a number of local potters' names and marks not before recorded. It was an interesting little discovery, and warrants the belief that regular excavations on the site would give valuable results. Indeed the whole place is strewn with relics of past glories. On the acropolis, now ploughed fields and shrub-covered slopes, are many standing ruins, one of which, a small temple built of brick and flint rubble, still bears traces of such delicate stucco reliefs as can be seen entire in the grottoes and buried vaults of Baiæ: the sunken lanes here have cut through the sewers and conduits of the vanished city, which show like giant rabbit-holes in the steep banks, and the ground above is littered with fragments of pottery and marble, and with the tesseræ of the broken mosaic floors. The village church, whose west front is a fine example of ornate Romanesque, is built almost entirely with Roman stones, and the clustered columns of its crypt, each with an ill-fitting capital of different pattern, all come from the classic ruins.

But though carved marble blocks and fragmentary inscriptions are scattered broadcast, yet this wreckage of Roman Cales will appeal to the ordinary traveller less than do the grotto-chapels of a later age. Two of these are in a deep valley below the acropolis; their entrances are screened and wellnigh blocked by fallen stones and trailing brambles; another, the best preserved, lies away to the far side of the village and is still in use; its floor is clear of debris and an iron door shields it from sacrilege. The sides of what was originally a natural cave have been straightened and squared, and on the walls are frescoes in the stiff style of Byzantine art. Nails have been driven at random into the rock to take the votive candles, whose smoke has played havoc with the rigid figures of saints arow round the dim chapel; the brilliant tints of their embroidered vestments have faded, the inscriptions above their heads are blackened and almost illegible, but there they stand in the severe formalism of their still enduring school, strangely modern, for you can see their like on the ikons of any Greek or Russian church of to-day, and as strangely old both by their setting and by the style so alien to our canons. The effect is perhaps most striking in the lowest valley shrine, where the sunlight thrusts in in splashes of green and gold through the veil of hanging leaves, where the rock-encumbered floor speaks of oblivion, and where the clustering wasp-cells and the bat-droppings give to the scaling walls that air of antiquity which one finds in Egypt's painted tombs. I know nothing of the date or history of those little chapels, nor what may be their interest to the student of Byzantine art, but to any lay traveller they are well worth a visit. For the classical ruins which crowd these Campanian foot-hills may grow wearisome by their surfeit, and it is a relief to turn from them and find in the painted grottoes of Calvi these livelier monuments of a more familiar faith.

But these excursions were perforce only too infrequent, and, for the most part, work at the baths claimed all my time. Venturi, my Tuscan servant, an invaluable fellow with a most un-Italian passion for cold baths and a genius for makeshift engineering, kept house for me in the palazzo and acted as foreman on the work. He would prepare our early breakfast, and soon after daybreak we would walk together to the diggings four miles away, where we would find our gang of some sixty men and girls eating their morning meal under the ruined vaults of the bath buildings. At mid-day we lunched in the farm close by, where an upper room served as office (and later as living-room for Venturi and myself), and at dusk we would walk back up the long white road to the town, turning aside religiously into a certain orange-garden where a wizened apple of an old rustic would hoe and prune, or, sitting on a fountain-basin backed by the weed-grown walls of the amphitheatre overlook the labours of his many children; then we would pick an orange each and pass the time of day with "old grandfather," and so on to the hostel in the town where we dined. It was a fairly strenuous life and at the end of the open-air day sleep came easily.

The scene of our work was a little valley planted

MASK OF A RIVER-GOD FROM THE TEANO BATHS.

ITALY

with poplars through which ran the stream that once supplied the baths. The bathing-rooms had occupied the low ground at the valley's bottom and were now buried deep in the silt of many freshets; a steep bank some thirty feet high rose on the left, and up this the ruins climbed in stairways and terraced chambers to the plateau above, whereon the façade of the building had stood fronting on the Roman road. These upper works had long since vanished, but in the bank's side there remained open to view walls and cave-like vaults of massive flint concrete; here the pitted surface of the cement showed how the ceilings had once been rich with glass mosaic, and strips and slabs of many-coloured marbles scattered over the ground bore further witness to the splendour that had been. But it was obvious that little save the ground-plan could be recovered from these weathered ruins exposed upon the slope; the statues and carvings which once adorned the entrance and the upper chambers must all have fallen into the wrack of rooms buried below the level ground which stretched from the bank's foot to the stream; here, therefore, most of our work was done, and it was with high hopes that we started, for the soil lay deep and undisturbed. But there was a factor with which we had not reckoned. The water of the stream possessed mineral qualities which doubtless built up the reputation of the ancient baths and were destined no less surely to complete their ruin. To the depth of some four feet the ground was fairly dry and objects found here were tolerably well preserved, but below this came the level of perpetual saturation and there the chemical action of the water had ruined everything. Slabs of coloured marble crumbled at a touch into red mud, white tesseræ from the mosaic floors ran liquid through one's fingers, and only a rust-red or green stain in the water-logged earth showed where metal had once lain. Our first experience of this corroding element was rather dramatic. About four feet below the surface we came upon the torso of a faun; it was lying face downwards, but the Praxitelean curve of the body and the careful working of the back muscles prepared us for a prize, so very cautiously the earth was scraped away all around and then, with the whole gang of workers clustering close in their excitement over the first " find," the figure was lifted up and a couple of bucketfuls of water thrown over it to wash away the mud that shrouded its front. As the mud ran off, the workmen started back with oaths of genuine dismay and the girls screamed or crossed themselves and ran, for, in place of the graceful faun we looked for, there lay before us a skeleton, and not cleanly bones at that, but an obscene thing about which still clung the rotting tatters of its marble flesh: the acids of the soil had eaten away all the soft parts of the stone to a depth of three or four inches, while the harder veins had resisted and stood out like the ragged framework of the white body. It was so grotesquely life-like—or death-like—that, quite apart from one's natural disappointment, one felt a real physical disgust at the sight of it, and we were only too glad to leave the thing to itself, face

STATUE OF CUPID FROM THE TEANO BATHS.

downwards, in the stable where our scanty finds were stored. It was the same with nearly everything which we unearthed here: inscriptions upon statue-bases or altars were illegible, fragments of sculpture could with difficulty be identified as such; and as soon as the ground-plan of the building could be made out I was obliged to abandon the work. Only two statues, lying in the upper soil, came out tolerably unscathed, one a rather coarse replica of the Capitoline Venus, headless and armless, which is now in the University Museum at Philadelphia, and the other, a pretty Cupid, veiled and flower-crowned, leaning on a column; the Cupid (see illustration), a pair to one in the Museo Baracco, which also came from the Teano baths, is now in the Naples Museum.

These two statues, which were found quite early in the course of the season, nearly involved me in serious trouble.

Permission had been asked for our work to begin on May 1, but when that date arrived the Naples Museum could spare none of its staff to act as the guardian or commissaire, who, according to Italian law, must be present at all excavations. Not wishing to lose time and good weather, we applied to the Minister at Rome for a special permit, and were told complacently enough that the law allowed experimental soundings to be made without the presence of a guard, and we might therefore begin at once, but must immediately report to the Ministry any finds of archæological importance which might be made during this trial stage. On May 1, therefore, I started work with my full gang, expecting the commissaire to turn up at any moment; actually it was not till the 23rd of the month, when things were in full swing, that the humble Museum guard, sent to keep watch over my doings, arrived in mufti at Teano station.

Naturally enough, he began by asking the stationmaster whether the English archæologist had yet arrived.

"Arrived?" replied that worthy; "why, for months he has been carrying on his work—work which is to enrich our artistic patrimony and restore to Teano its ancient glory!"

The astonished guard tried to insist that digging could not have begun already, but the stationmaster was not to be shaken, so, having learnt that I was probably to be found at the little inn where I always dined, the now-thoroughly disturbed official took a carriage and drove up the long dusty road to Teano. On arriving at the *trattoria* he was told by the innkeeper that I was then, as every day, down at the excavations.

"But have the excavations really started?"

"Started indeed! but they are enormous! and such discoveries!" (this with the gusto of one who had never been near them), "such magnificent statues, such grandiose ruins!"

This was too much. Hurriedly donning his uniform and girding on a heavy revolver, the guard drove at full speed down to the farm and appeared on the scene just as we had laid our new-found Venus by

ITALY

the stream's side and were washing the earth from off her marble limbs. Then pandemonium broke. Inarticulate with rage, but shouting lustily, the guard drew his revolver and began brandishing it in unpleasant proximity to my head; the women screamed, the workmen seized their picks and advanced to the rescue, while the guard, recovering a little his wits, shouted that all work must stop, that all of us were under arrest, that he forbade a man to move, or me to speak, that he forbade everything.

By a mere chance I had been amusing myself that morning with some revolver practice, so, taking advantage of a more than usually splendid gesticulation in which both of the official's hands were involved, I drew the weapon and, putting it to his head, persuaded him by his own argument to keep quiet; at the same time I ordered the men to stop work, assuring them that it was all a mistake, but that the representative of the law must be obeyed; and then, when things were calmer and our respective weapons back in their holsters, I began to reason with him. My first argument was that I was engaged in such "soundings" as the law explicitly allowed, but he only snorted and, pointing to my sixty work-people and half an acre of deep trenches, dismissed the definition: these were excavations, carried on in his absence and therefore illegal, and now all was to be stopped, and he would wire to the Ministry at Rome denouncing me. I then urged that as we had been expecting all along the permission which had now admittedly been given, we should never have been such fools as to compromise ourselves by an illegal act—in fact we had an understanding with the Minister for everything. The guard replied that he knew of no such understanding. I retorted that he, naturally, was not in the secrets of the Ministry, but would certainly get into trouble if he disregarded them; he grew obstinate, did not care about arrangements of which he had not been informed, and was determined on doing his duty. Upon this I at once became sympathetic, agreed that he ought indeed to report me, and only regretted the trouble that he was bringing on his own head.

"What trouble?" he demanded, obviously taken aback by my change of tone; "it's only my duty that I'm doing."

"Precisely," said I, "that is the danger. Do you realize where and what you are?"

"I am an official of the Italian Government——'

"Yes, and where?"

He was puzzled, then said, "Why, in South Italy, of course."

"And did you ever know of a Government official who, in the south of Italy, did his duty and did not get into trouble?"

That settled it. "Never!" he said, with a sigh. "Please, Signor Professore, would you tell me what I had better do?"

In the end I telegraphed for instructions myself the poor guard received an official answer which brought him to me in tears, and I got a request to

GROUP OF WORKPEOPLE AT THE BATHS, TEANO.
On the Author's right is the Government Commissaire, on his left Venturi.

report regularly on his conduct, together with the offer to recoup myself for lost working hours out of his scanty wage. I did not explain to him that my telegram and the answers to it had passed through somewhat devious channels, but I did send in an encomium on his character (I was careful to show it to him first) which made the much-wronged man the most obliging of commissaires.

In those days, indeed, it was wise—perhaps it still is—to have the Camorra on one's side, though, so far as I remember, the above was the only occasion on which I made direct use of it. Already that great criminal organization was in its decline, and its weak-kneed leader had been stabbed to death by his lieutenants in the sunken lane that winds between Resina's vineyards; but the great trial of the murderers, a trial which was to shake Southern Italy to its core, had not yet taken place, and most people still believed that no Government would dare to put the Camorrists in the dock. Naples had, in fact, but just enjoyed a good illustration of the Society's power. Tired of the extortionate ways of the Neapolitan cabby, which affected disastrously the tourist traffic of the town, the Municipality had decided to introduce taximeters and to grant licences to no cabs that did not carry such. Tenders for the supply of taximeters had been received from two firms, and the Council had met to assign the contract and to fix the date by which the new regulation was to come into force, when the President announced that he had received a letter which he felt obliged to lay before the Council before proceeding to the business in hand. The letter was from the Camorra: it spoke with approval of the new law, agreed as to the benefits it would confer on the Municipality, the tourists, and the contracting firms, but expressed inability to see "where the Camorra came in"; the writer proposed, therefore, that a gratification of so many thousand liras should be paid in advance to the secretary of the Society, to which should be added annually a fixed tariff on each taximeter in use "which you might enter in your books," he remarked "as payment for the life of drivers using such machines." The Municipality accepted the proposal and the money was duly paid.

I had come down to Naples once for a week-end when Baron Zarone, meeting me in the Club, began to ask how I was getting on in the quarters he had lent me in his palazzo at Teano. I told him that was very comfortable except for one thing, but that that was so serious as to drive me to distraction Quite upset, and believing that I was in earnest the Baron demanded what this could be. I told him that, some ten days before, I was awakened at about half-past three in the morning by a terrific din in the palace courtyard, on to which opened the tall French windows of my bedroom; as the noise went on got out of bed and, running to the window, could just see in the half-light of the early day an old man who stood below me in the courtyard and bellowed "Giuseppe, Giuseppe," as though to wake the dead When I asked him what he wanted, he stopped his bellowing for a moment to explain that it was a Saint's Day, and Giuseppe, who was not dead but asleep in a garret somewhere above my head, was wanted to help ring the church bells. Then he began again, but I used such a flow of good Neapolitan— and Neapolitan is a rich *argot* to swear in—that he took to his heels and left me to a peaceful if a sleepless pillow. But a few days later another Saint's Day came, and the nuisance was repeated, and this time the old man, strong in the righteousness of his cause, refused to be alarmed by my oaths, and woke Giuseppe, even at the cost of an hour's yelling. Then it happened a third time. "My dear Baron," I said, "it is too much. I go to bed tired, and if wakened by this horrible noise I can't sleep any more: the strain is telling on my health, and as there is a whole string of Saints' Days coming on next week, I shall probably die." The old gentleman was full of regrets, though barren of remedies; but an acquaintance of mine, a prominent Camorrista, who, standing close by, had overheard my tragic story, was at once ready with a suggestion. "Go down and shoot the fellow," he said.

"My dear sir," I retorted, "there's nothing I should like better, but a pistol-shot at 3.30 A.M. attracts attention, and the police-station is just against the door of the palace courtyard. What should I do if a policeman came in and found a dead bell-ringer on the ground and me standing over him with a revolver still smoking in my hand?"

"What should you do?" answered the Camorrista;

"why, that is quite simple; just give the policeman a couple of francs and mention my name!"

I believe that my friend's confidence was genuine though perhaps exaggerated, but I was not likely to act on it. However, when next the old sexton started to make morning hideous, I did run down with a revolver and therewith emphasized my desire for silence; and he certainly took the threat seriously judging by the speed with which he scuttled. Only once more during my stay at Teano did I hear him call Giuseppe to the belfry—and then, waking by chance, I caught pathetically faint from some far alley-way behind the palazzo a wail which could surely have evoked no answer but a snore.

As a matter of fact, pistol-shots were not altogether uncommon when of an evening things grew lively in the town; but I never heard of an arrest resulting from them, and it was only an incident down near the diggings that explained for me this immunity for violence. Beyond the "fundo" where were my field headquarters lived an elderly farmer, a fat, jovial man who used often to come to the valley of the baths and watch our work. He spent most of his time wandering about with two dogs and a gun in pursuit of hares, assured me that a hare *had* been seen on his farm once, but pending its reappearance contented himself with shooting cuckoos, whose call he imitated well enough to bring them within a few yards of him. One day I was told that his son, while walking out with his sweetheart, had quarrelled with her over the question of going to America, and in his rage had stabbed her three times and thrown her body into a ditch; so, meeting the old fellow on his rounds, I ventured to sympathize with him on this domestic "disgrazia." But he did not seem at all depressed. "The girl is not dead," he said; "in fact, I don't think she's going to die, so it will be all right."

"And your son?" I asked.

"Oh, he's in hiding."

"What! taken to the hills, I suppose?"

"No, no, he's down at the house; but of course he is keeping indoors for a day or two."

A good deal puzzled, I pushed my inquiries further, and learnt that in cases of murderous assault the police are supposed to hunt down and arrest the assailant; but if at the end of three days he is still at large and the victim still alive, the criminal charge is dropped, nor are the police further interested in the matter, unless the assaulted party takes out a warrant, which, fearing a repetition of the attack, he very seldom does. So when the assault has not proved fatal, it is obviously simpler for the police to reduce their investigations to a mere pretence, and after three days be quit of the whole troublesome business. In this Teano case the young man was soon going freely about his business, and as the lady recovered and was so forgiving as to marry him, the system after all may be said to have been justified by its happy results!

Pleasant as life was in the palazzo at Teano, the town lay too far from the work to be really convenient, and at a later stage of the dig I moved down and took up my abode in the farmhouse close to the baths. Here Venturi and I shared the upper room, which was approached by an out-of-door stone staircase, the invariable feature of these southern "fundi," and the farmer's wife cooked our simple meals in the great room on the ground-floor, which served at once as kitchen, sleeping-room for the whole family, and fowls' run. They were good simple folk—the farmer with long whiskers drooping to sparse points of faded brown; his wife, a thin flat-chested woman, with anxious deeply-lined face and an inexhaustible energy; and their strapping daughter, who worked in the fields and cooked or did the rare redding of the house in the intervals of out-door work. Often of an evening I would sit with them in front of the open hearth—I and any labourer who chanced to have overstayed his time—talking of village gossip, the crops, or, for it is still living subject there, the divine right of the Borbon kings. They were much interested in the diggings too, and deeply grieved at the poor success of them. One day, I remember, a sudden rainstorm had driven us into the kitchen, and Zarone's factor, a fine old countryman, Giuseppe Caianello by name, was lamenting our scanty finds, when the farmer's wife assured him that my luck would soon turn—oh, it would turn beyond a doubt, for she had but that morning hung above my bed a coloured picture of Sant' Antonio, and he was a lucky saint if ever there was one!

"Sant' Antonio?" retorted Caianello with deep contempt; "and what, pray, is the use of Sant' Antonio? You hail from Bari way, and of course over there he may be all right, but he's got no power in these parts! If you want anything here you must go to San Paridi."

"But who is San Paridi?" asked the "padrona," who was in truth a foreigner.

"Well, he's the only saint who counts for much hereabouts, and a good one for your money too. It's his picture you ought to put up over the Eccellenza's bed."

The goodwife sought further enlightenment, and as the rain showed no signs of stopping, "'o fattor'" settled himself at ease, relit his cheroot, and related the veracious story of Teano's saint. It was a long yarn, full of digressions, of contradictions, and of gaps, and told in an *argot* none too easy to follow, but as well as I can remember it, it ran thus:

"Ecco: Signor Paridi—he was no saint then, but a poor man, though book-learned—he lived long ago at Teano, very long ago, before ever our Lord Christ was born, and he was a Saracen by race, and a pagan; and because of his learning he became a sorcerer too. Now at that time there was at Teano a Dragon which lived in a cave and ate men and laid waste all the country. You know where the road from Teano on its way past here crosses the river valley by the bridge? Well, it was in that valley the Dragon lived, in the cave in the cliff there; and out of that cave he used to come and kill folk on the road, and right up to the town, and all, the world was afraid of him. And Dom Paridi, who was a good man, though a Saracen, was sorry for the people, so he came down to the cave where the Dragon was, and, so they say, he turned himself into a dragon too—for no mortal man could have stood up against a beast like that; but anyhow he fought the Dragon and killed him, and saved all the country. And that's true enough, for there's his chapel to this day, standing just below the bridge and in part of the Dragon's cave, as you can see it for yourself. After that, of course, the people thought a lot of Dom Paridi, and talked about him and what he had done, until news of it came to the king. For in those days there was a king in these parts, and he was a Saracen too, and a bad lot. He had a great park with a wall all round it full of live tigers, and if a man did wrong, or if the king just didn't like any one, he'd take him and throw him over the wall to the tigers, and they ate him up,—the king, Saracen that he was, watching all the time over the top of the wall. Lots of people he treated like that, and they say you could hardly see the grass in the park for the bones that lay about in it. Well, as I was saying, news came to the king that Dom Paridi was a great sorcerer, more powerful than the king himself, and that he could change himself into a tiger or anything else he pleased. Now sorcery was a forbidden thing in those times, so the king sent the carabinieri and arrested Dom Paridi and brought him to the park and threw him over, *povero disgraziato*, into the middle of the tigers. The king himself was sitting on the wall to watch, for he thought that Dom Paridi would change himself into a tiger, but that the real tigers would see that he wasn't a proper one at all, and so would be more savage than ever and eat him up quick. But Dom Paridi didn't. He just remained a man as he was, and all the tigers came up and—what do you think? —they all went down on their knees to him and said their aves and their paternosters, and him standing in the middle of them! Then of course the king knew that he wasn't a bad man at all, and so he took him out of the park and gave him a job under the government, next to the king's self. So Dom Paridi became a very great man and ruled the country round here: and after that our Signor Jesu was born, and Dom Paridi became a great saint for all Teano, though he was a Saracen up till then, and the only Saracen that ever was a saint. So if you want anything done here in Teano you go to San Paridi, and let Sant' Antonio look after Bari and those parts."

The farmer's wife agreed that a saint who was a Saracen and lived before the coming of Christ must be a very fine saint, and two or three days later San Paradi, dragon and all, took the place of Saint Antony over my bed; but to every one's astonishment my luck underwent no change for the better!

The religious ideas of these southern peasants are delightfully simple. Many of them are more than a little suspicious of their priests as such — and the ignorant pedantry of these latter too often warrants the suspicion—but in the Faith itself they have that profound belief to which the perverseness of the Southern temper aptly witnesses. Just as the oath " per la Madonna che m' a creato " (" By the Madonna who made me ") gives weight to the most common lie, so when things go wrong and tempers are lost the Meridionale reserves his coarsest invective for the Virgin; it is the fervency of his belief that gives point to his blasphemy. " Black-jowled humbug," the peasant will murmur as the priest meets him in the road, and will cross himself devoutly as soon as he has passed: the curse is for the man and the system, the gesture for the faith behind it.

Two of the best of these free-thinking, pious Southerners I got to know during a short time I spent once exploring in the valley of the Sabato, where there are some ruins which writers in Italian journals had tried to identify with the birthplace of the ancient Sabines. A journey by train up from Naples through the foot-hills of Northern Calabria, and then a tramp from the little station, brought me to Serino, a valley of deep, bubbling springs whence Naples draws its water-supply, the best water, perhaps, that any great city boasts; then came a long trek up along the valley, across water-courses and through beech woods, till, the last little hamlet left a good five miles behind, we climbed the hill-side to the ramshackle two-roomed cabin which I was to share with my companions, hosts, and servants. These were two forest-rangers, hardy open livers, who knew nothing of the lands beyond their woods and mountains. One was a young fellow, handsome of face, supple of body as a lynx, and a great dandy to boot with his long love-locks, his finely-curled moustache, heavy gold earrings, a gaudy silk kerchief for his neck, and brown velvet corduroys like the sleek brown fur of a wood animal. The other, a grizzled veteran, remembered the old days when robbers and outlaws infested all the hills, and a forest ranger had need be featly with his gun if he was to keep a sound skin. His father, a ranger before him, had died in such a way. "It was in the early morning, eccellenz', with a mist over the upper rocks, and my father saw three of them at once coming towards him. So he got down behind a big stone, and with three shots he killed all three. Ah! he was a true master of the gun, and he loading between each shot; but there were five others there whom he had not seen, so they killed him, and because he had shot so well they carried him down to the house, and we buried the four all together. So went things under the Borbone, eccellenz'."

Our life in the Sabato valley was simple to an extreme. We got up before daybreak, drank a cup of coffee, and went off to the work; lunch was served in the hut shortly after noon— macaroni and bread, cherries, and a bottle of wine; then out on the work till dusk, and at any time between seven and eight we three, together with any of the workmen who might prefer to stop the night with us, sat down to an equally plain meal of thin bovril soup, a dish of the golden-brown fungi that clustered round the chestnut boles, bread, and a couple of bottles each of the same rough red wine, and then over more wine and cigarettes we would sit and talk till heads nodded for bedtime. Once in answer to some jest the elder ranger with a " Funny dog," smote his young companion on the shoulder just too hard, and in a flash knives were out, and I had to jump in to make peace. Once the old topic of the king of Naples and the disastrous effects of a United Italy almost led to bloodshed: but for the most part they were splendid rambling talks, wherein past times met and mingled with the present—which in that lonely valley showed so little change—and I spoke of Egypt, maybe, or of England, and they of their woods and hills and of the evils of emigration, of landlords, and of the priesthood, and of the faith that was above the priests. "What, is everything then that we are told in church a lie?" demanded the younger man once when my phrase " B.C." had seemed to him to clash with the priest's description of Christ as "The First Man," nor would anything persuade him that the words were meant in other than a literal sense. "No, it was a lie; but thank God we don't depend for the Madonna upon them!"

On another occasion as we sat drinking together I turned to the older forester, and recalling our first meeting, which had been in the village street of Serino on the evening of the last Sunday in May, I said, quizzing him, "Do you remember that you said to me then, 'Of course you are going to church,' and we all went together, for it was the feast of the Madonna? Now, why did you say 'of course'?"

"Ebbene," replied he, "it was a day when all good Catholics would go to church, and I saw you were a good Catholic."

"But how could you see that?"

"How? but really, eccellenz', that's simple enough!"

"I shouldn't call it so, anyhow; tell me how you knew."

The old man glanced up sharply to see whether I was making fun of him, but since I looked serious enough, he went on with a rather laboured patience to explain his system.

"After all's said and done," said he, "there are only three sorts of people in the world — good Catholics, atheists, and pagans, and as I could see you were neither of the last two, I knew you must be of the first."

"But *how* did you know? What's the difference in the looks of them?"

"Oh, come now," he said simply, "good Catholics, why, they're just ordinary people like you and me; and as for atheists, it's stamped on their faces that they're damned already in this world, to say nothing of the next. And pagans are black!"

The ruins I had come to examine, rough walls of concrete and rubble encircling some acres of wooded hill-top, were not indeed the cradle of the old Sabine race, but dated from well on in the Christian age, and seemed rather to have been a place of refuge to which the villagers might betake themselves and their cattle for shelter, perhaps, in those parlous times when Alaric turned southwards after the sack of Rome and when the long-drawn war between Goth and Latin gave rein to anarchy in the unguarded hills. From the point of view of the archæologist, these late and nameless ruins had little to recommend them, but no one could ask for a fairer working-ground. The rounded hillock which the ramparts crowned rose steeply from the river-bed, and was joined to the true foot-hills of the valley-side by a narrow saddle which led to the one gateway in the wall's whole circuit. Great beech trees covered the downward slope, beech trees and chestnuts mingled on the hill-top, and from here one looked northward along the straight valley where the stream ran, low in those summer days, between its broken banks with here and there beside it a narrow strip of tilth or grassland and patches of cherry trees half smothered in the thick chestnut scrub which clothed the lower slopes. A little higher up on either side the chestnuts gave way to oaks, and these again to darker pines, while towering abrupt above the pine-tops stood the cliff which like a marble wall shut in the valley and hid all but the highest snow-clad peaks beyond. And with all this, in all this clear-cut distance, not a house to be seen; only, perhaps, for sign of man, a slender spire of smoke would be rising from the chestnut copses where the

THE ENCEINTE WALL OF LA CIVITA IN THE VALLEY OF THE SABATO, SHOWING THE GATEWAY ON THE LEFT.

charcoal-burners were at work. The deserts of Nubia were not more out of the world than this valley of the upper Sabato, but in place of parched land and sun-split rock here were running water, grass, and trees and mountains, few but kindly human folk about one, and glimpses surely of Pan and the woodland sprites in tangled gullies and on long-shadowed lawns.

At about eight o'clock of a morning my workmen would stop for breakfast, while I, instead of eating, would stroll round or sit and smoke, looking at the view up the valley. But one day at that time I saw one of the gang, who had cut the early hours of work, come running and jumping down the hillside to the great gateway, swinging as he came a half-filled goatskin; it was fresh mountain milk which he was churning in this rough and ready fashion, and coming up to where I sat, he undid the skin and showed me the white creamy cheese already separated from the whey. Then he squeezed it between bracken-fronds to strain it, and while others hurried up with cherries, red wine, and bread, he whittled a spoon for the soft cheese out of a fresh beech branch, and found broad dock-leaves for a plate. I ate my breakfast there on the slope above the river, the men, a little way apart, laughing and singing sometimes a snatch of song over their wine; and unseen in the woods below me a goat-boy played on his pipe of single reed an air older than Rome, older than the Sabine hill-towns, the air which the wind sings to the rocks and shrubs of upland pastures.

CARCHEMISH

I HAVE proposed to write of the lighter side of our work, and to leave archæology in the background, but since in all tales the background must needs count for something, let me say a little about the scene in which are cast many of the events that follow. I have no intention of giving a laboured description of Carchemish, and indeed the time is not yet ripe to do so, seeing that many seasons' work must be completed before we can draw a detailed picture of this old city of temples and palaces; but it were not out of place briefly to sketch both the present appearance of its site and the ruins which our workmen are unearthing. Jerablus seems so remote, and the Hittite power whose capital Carchemish was is so strange to most, that without some such foreword the stories to be told and the men of whom I shall speak would seem isolated from all reality, lacking altogether the natural setting of landscape and labour.

Yet, thanks to modern railways, to get to Jerablus is nowadays a very simple matter. From the harbour of Beirut the train takes you in sharp zigzags and up improbable gradients across the range of Lebanon to Rayak, where you change to the broad-gauge line that runs through the Orontes valley to Aleppo. You pass Baalbek, the village hidden behind its groves of poplars and fruit trees, and the glorious columns of its Sun Temple silhouetted against the sky, a mere tantalizing glimpse of them caught through the greenery to reproach you if you have not spent the day there. You pass Homs, first the lake on your left with, on its far bank, the great mound of Kadesh where Rameses III fought that doubtful battle which his poets turned to victory, and then on your right the town, hidden altogether until your train curls round on to the lip of the hollow wherein it lies, with its citadel-mound rising in the midst and the ruins of Roman buildings reaching up to the railway line to remind you of the crazy Syrian boy Elagabalus who here made such love to the Roman legions as to become Emperor of Rome and a byword for evil living. You cross Orontes and you come to Hama with its gardens and giant water-wheels, and so on over rolling steppes of rich red earth till in mid-afternoon a great embattled castle leaps above the horizon and you wind round a little river valley to Aleppo. There you will stop the night—or more than one, if you be not too squeamish about your lodging, for there is much to see in the great town—and then from the new station on the Bagdad railway a run of four hours or so will bring you to Jerablus and the Euphrates.

From the railway station the fields slope gently

down towards the river, the gradual fall broken halfway by a long grass-clad mound which rises steeply as earth will stand from a shallow trench; the rough track heads for a V-shaped notch in the middle of the mound's line, and when you pass through this you are in Carchemish. The long earthwork is the city wall, the gap through which you came is the western gate, around you lie the scattered stones of the ruined town, and in front, dominating all, is the scarred bulk of the acropolis.

The city lay low upon the river bank, and, owing to the downward trend of the land beyond its limits, the site does not at first glance seem particularly well chosen; from the plateau where the station is, all appears dwarfed, commanded too easily from this vantage-point of shelving hill. But climb the great mound of the acropolis, and you will understand at once why Carchemish was from immemorial time a fortress in a troubled land.

Beneath your feet a little stream runs from the west into the Euphrates; to-day it is but a narrow runlet, most of whose waters are taken up by a millsluice and by irrigation channels that tap it near its source and skirt the upper slopes of its fertile little valley; but near its mouth the banks are high and steep, and it may well be that four thousand years ago its waters were enough to make a formidable barrier. But the angle made by the two rivers had another advantage, for at its point is a rocky outcrop which, starting as a steep cliff over the tributary's southern bank, swelled then into a

CARCHEMISH: GENERAL VIEW OF THE EXCAVATIONS (1913).

In the left foreground is the great Stairway and the Long Wall of Sculpture, the slabs still lying as they were found; beyond this, the Royal buttress of the Processional Entry. In the middle background is the expedition house, behind it the barracks and hospital of the Bagdad Railway; in the left distance the village of Jerablus.

hummock a hundred feet or more in height, with abrupt sides above the main stream of the Euphrates, sloping more gently but steeply yet to landward, and ending in a broken tongue of rock at its southern end. To the primitive castle-builder this was an ideal site. Defended on two sides by water, with difficulty accessible from the land, it needed but little in the way of walls to make of it a fortress impregnable, and as such it was early chosen and continued long in use. Starting at the top of the mound, we have dug down over fifty feet through the accumulated debris of the ages, and still human remains meet us. Arab huts, only just hidden by the grass, give place to Armenian; beneath these are Byzantine ruins, stratum below stratum, three or four building periods to be distinguished in a few feet's depth; then the scanty remains of the Roman fort which one of the Legions built to secure Europus ford; then Greek things dating from the Roman time back to the second century B.C. Below these comes Carchemish of the Hittites, again marked off into distinct levels and periods, of which the latest is the fort built or remodelled by Sargon the Assyrian when in 717 B.C., after nearly half a century of war, he had captured the capital of the Hittite Empire, and the earliest may date back to 2000 or 2500 B.C. Four thousand years of history, of sieges, and of changing population, and we are yet only some twenty feet down in the great mound; behind these centuries stretches the incalculable period of the prehistoric age. In the sides of our trenches, below the lowest Hittite floor-level, you can see mud-brick walls and floors of beaten earth; under the floors the graves of those who once lived here, skeletons laid out at length in stone cists crowded with clay vessels of offerings, and farther down broken bones in jars, types of burial differing with the ages—but still the walls go down and down. Now flint implements and weapons are found in the floors or in the rubbish between the walls, and fragments of brightly-painted neolithic pottery show up in contrast to the drab waves of the upper strata: there is the whole history of Carchemish in that earth cutting. But here, thirty or fifty feet down, we can speak no more of dates nor calculate the lapse of time; the workers of the Stone Age who first held the fort on the rocky promontory came before the beginnings of history, and how long since they lived and died we have no means of telling.

The view from the top of the Kala'at or Fortress Mound is very fine. Immediately below you runs the Euphrates, in spring-time when the floods are out a turbid mass of brown water leaping and eddying, a thousand yards across, in summer less impressive but more beautiful, for then green islands, flower-dotted, rise above the surface, and the divided stream runs rippling through many channels, and only at the mound's foot the main current, four hundred yards wide, is still deep and fast. Just opposite is the village of Zormara, its fields and orchards set against a background of low grey-green hills, the edge of the Mesopotamian

CARCHEMISH: THE EXPEDITION HOUSE FROM THE CITY WALL.

In the middle distance is seen the Euphrates with the temporary wooden bridge of the Bagdad Railway; across the river (on the left) are the houses and gardens of Zormara.

CARCHEMISH 79

steppes, which to north and south close in upon the river and fall in cliffs of red-brown earth straight to the water. Northward lies rolling ground upon the right bank, with one or two villages half seen in the folds, and on the left the limestone cliffs and sharper hill-contours this side of Birijik. Southwards you look over the rich plains where Pharaoh Necho fought his great battle against Assyria in 605 B.C.; at its upper end, close outside the city's walls, is the new railway, with the great bridge spanning the Euphrates; beyond that the village of Jerablus, and cornfields and hamlets stretching away to where the limestone hills sweep round again to meet the river; just on their edge you can see the fortress-mound of Tell Amarna, another Hittite stronghold securing the lower end of the rich valley, and on the far bank another "Tell," that of lower Shukh, and right away near the horizon the mound of Tell Ahmar, the ancient Til Barsip, by whose possession Shalmaneser II of Assyria made himself master of the Euphrates ford.

Stretching along the river, between the mound's foot and the railway, lies the ruin-strewn site of the old city girt about by its earthen walls. In the earlier stages of our work, when Hittite remains were comparatively few, that which most struck the eye, looking down thus upon the Kala'at's whole expanse, was the wreckage of Roman Europus. From the south gateway, whose massive jambs still stood three feet high or so above the scattered debris in the gap of the earth rampart, a long straight street ran almost to the foot of the acropolis. Lines of masonry, with column bases here and there and the broken shafts of the great colonnade, marked its course across the grass; on the edge of the side-walk were the shop-fronts with their long narrow grooves into which the shutters were let down at night; here was the curved wall of a basilica apse, here fragments of moulded architrave with boldly-cut letters spelling out the titles of Cæsar. The gateway has been cleared away now to lay bare the Hittite gate beneath, and many of the walls have also had to go. Though one make beforehand all such records as plans and photographs and writing will afford, it is a sorry task to demolish finally these ruins which have so long defied the wastage of time, and especially so to one who has worked on Roman sites in England where these things would in themselves amply repay a season's labour; but such destruction is unavoidable where one city overlies another and the lower strata are the more precious. Of course nothing is destroyed except in the sure and certain hope of finding something better underneath, and there is at least comfort in the thought that in North Syria there are perhaps a hundred sites where Roman towns stand better preserved than at Carchemish and where no lower levels of discovery need cause their overthrow.

I must admit that unwillingness to remove these Roman buildings is increased at the start and alloyed with exasperation as work goes forward by their remarkable solidity. To find a promising Hittite

SKETCH PLAN
of
CARCHEMISH.

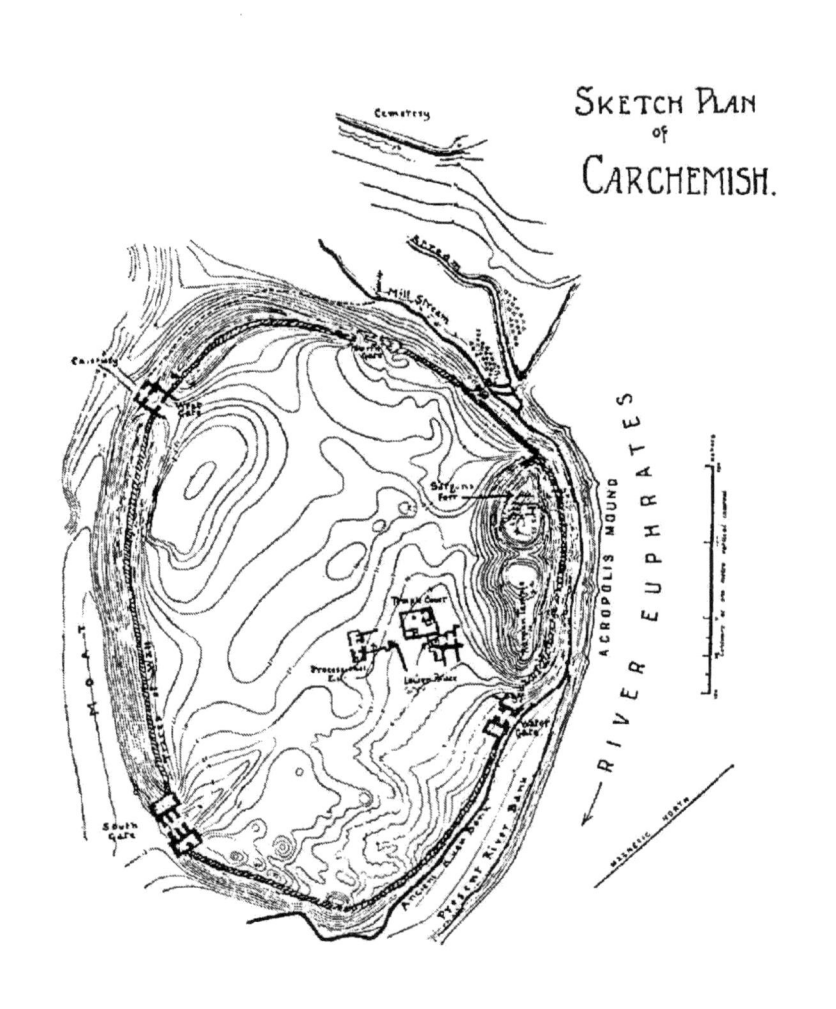

area overlaid by beds of concrete twenty feet across and six or seven feet thick, concrete as hard to-day as when the lime and flint were first mixed, and capped with building-stones each a yard square,—this is enough to irritate the mildest temper, and one takes a malicious pleasure in carting off the last fragments of what one first attacked with genuine regret. Sometimes a length of wall, concrete foundations and heavy masonry, may be cautiously undercut until the earth trickles from beneath it in warning and the men are called away, and the whole will come crashing down in fragments on the Hittite pavement: more often blasting must be employed, and this, too, needs careful work, for the Romans not infrequently threw in Hittite sculptures as a foundation for their concrete, and this must be broken up by the charge without damage to what it may conceal; so it is a slow and a laborious job, and one is thankful when the last truck-load of jagged Roman stuff is tilted into the river and the picks can turn again to deal with kindly earth.

. . . . .

It is not Roman Europus but Carchemish of the Hittites with which our work is concerned, and of this what remains? First, the acropolis mound and the great walls, and then the buildings which are slowly coming to light in the cleared area just below the mound, and the gates that break the wall's line.

Of the acropolis itself little need be said. The great mound has two crests, joined by a narrow and lower neck: on the north-eastern summit the fort built by Sargon has demolished most of what was there before it—at least we have not yet gone deep enough below to speak of older work,—and on the south-west the concrete foundations of a Roman temple, dating from the second century A.D., are cut down into the neolithic levels, and have left little of true Hittite work. Only the ring-wall of the Hittite fortress can be traced, on the river front a single massive rampart high up on the steep face of the rock, to landward a series of descending terraces, not unlike the *Ziggurat* of Babylonian sites.

A breastwork, zigzagged up the steep slope, linked the keep to the outer wall of the city. On the north side, where the steep banks of the little stream gave natural defence, there was no earth mound, and the wall of masonry and brick rose directly from ground-level: most of it has perished, and only one massive buttress still stands intact on the grassy flat above the mill; and of the northern gateway, too, where-through the road led to the bridge (or earlier to the ford across the stream), only faint traces now remain. From where the gateway was, the mound begins rising steadily to the north-west corner, and thence runs at full height along the western front. Here where the ground sloped downward towards the town, the works of man had to make good the shortcomings of nature. A great ditch with sharply-sloping sides was therefore dug southwards from the mill-stream, whose waters filled its lower depths: thirty feet deep the ditch was cut into soil and rock, and the

CLEARING SARGON'S FORT ON THE TOP OF THE ACROPOLIS MOUND

CARCHEMISH

earth thrown up upon its inner edge made a mound sixty feet high from base to crest, and above this towered the wall proper. To-day the ditch has been wellnigh filled up, and of the builded wall only a few rough foundation-stones remain, but the great earthwork still stands to its full height, and is the first thing to challenge the attention of the visitor. Seen from the inside, where the debris of countless buildings has raised the ground-level far above what it once was, the walls are not very imposing, but from the outside the steep grass-grown mound looms high and forbidding: certainly when the wall stood with its towers and battlements complete and the water glistened in the moat below, this was a barrier that may well have defied the hosts of Assyria throughout forty years of siege.

Midway along the western front was a gate approached by a causeway of rock, left when the rest was cut away to make the moat. There were three pairs of folding-doors with guard-chambers in between, and lofty towers of stone and brick flanked the entrance. Here was the vulnerable point in the defences, and here we found signs of tragedy. The outer gateways with their buttresses had been razed to the ground, and athwart the jambs of the inner door a solid mass of brickwork had been built to close the entrance. The slipshod style of the brickwork spoke of haste, and bones and fragments of armour found in the rubbish piled in front of it would seem to show that the barrier was thrown up under stress of war; a signet engraved in the very latest

Hittite style was also found here, and we may well see in this rough blocking of the road a desperate shift employed when Sargon's army was encamped on the level ground beyond the walls, and his rams had breached the gate, and the end of the long war hung imminent over Carchemish.

The south gate was far better preserved than the western, and more than compensated for the destruction of the Greek and Roman structures which overlay it. It was of massive ashlar masonry up to a height of ten or twelve feet, with brickwork above: the corners of its flanking towers were guarded by lions, their bodies carved in high relief, while their heads, cut in the round, projected beyond the outer angles of the towers: a colossal statue in hard limestone adorned the entrance, a seated figure apparently, whose head and shoulders alone survive the hammers of Babylonian iconoclasts, but once a masterpiece of Hittite sculpture. The ground-plan of the triple gateway is now clear to see, with the stone hinge-sockets still in place, the recesses into which the doors folded back, the guard-chambers in the flanking towers, and the stairway to the battlements: it needs but little imagination to reconstruct the whole, and to see before one the gates of Carchemish as they stood in their prime.

Along the river front there was no mound, for the Euphrates was defence sufficient in itself: only on the water's edge rose the stone wall whose foundations can still be traced in the gathered silt of the bank. Just below the acropolis mound was another gateway, the water-gate, opening on a quay, and serving less for

CARCHEMISH: THE GATEWAY OF THE PROCESSIONAL ENTRY.

defence than for pageantry; unlike the rest, therefore, it was a monumental work richly adorned with carvings in limestone and basalt.

In all Hittite buildings of the better class the lowest part of the walling, to a height of three feet or so, is faced with stone slabs, a podium as it were, on which rests the brickwork of the upper courses. Sometimes these slabs are plain, sometimes covered with inscriptions or reliefs, and where this is the case the architect often preferred to use blocks of basalt and of limestone alternately, thus giving a black-and-white effect which is distinctly pleasing and original. The style of the carving makes it tolerably certain that the white limestone reliefs were coloured: perhaps the basalt slabs too were touched up with paint, just as the Egyptians touched up their dark granite sculptures: the polychrome scheme must have been most gorgeous, how gorgeous it is difficult to realize to-day, when the soft outlines and flattened planes of the limestone sculptures tend to make them somewhat feeble, and only the sharp-cut basalt figures preserve their due balance of light and shade.

The water-gate is built in this black-and-white style. The rain-water flooding down the Kala'at sides has scarred this part of the site, and laid bare the Hittite levels, so that some of the gate-reliefs were above ground before we started work, and these are so weathered and lichen-grown as to be but the ghosts of their old selves; other slabs and fragments of sculptures were found tumbled from the old quay edge and buried in the river bank; by the measurements of these and on the analogy of the Hittite gateway at Sakjegeuzi we were, however, able to reconstruct the whole scheme of the entrance, though the north side of it has perished altogether. A sloping road broken by steps led from the quay between rows of sculpture. At the corner of the river-wall was a lion, then came bulls and lions again, and the group of guardian demons proper to a gateway—an architectural amulet, as it were, to keep evil spirits from the entrance; there is a scene of sacrifice, a bull and a goat led to the slaughter, and a seated priest or king who pours libations to the gods. The outer door-jambs were formed by huge basalt lions carved in the round, and measuring twelve feet from head to tail, with a long inscription carved upon their flanks. To-day the gateway is a battered ruin, contrasting poorly indeed with the buildings inside the town; but apart from the picture which it enables us to draw of what it was in palmier days, it has a historical importance which the better-preserved ruins lack. There are two main periods to be observed in Carchemish city, an earlier and truly Hittite period, dating back to anything between 1500 and 2000 B.C., and, separated from this by a phase of destruction and decay, a later period in which the temples and palaces were rebuilt or re-embellished on a grander scale: this era of prosperity and of corresponding artistic wealth comes after 1200 B.C., and is due to the infusion of new blood, probably to the preponderance of those

CARCHEMISH: THE LONG WALL OF SCULPTURE ENCLOSING THE TEMPLE COURT BELOW THE GREAT STAIRCASE.

The slabs have been replaced in position and the wall restored in mud brick.

Mushki folk about whom we know as yet so little. The water-gate was one of the structures remodelled in this later period, but the new building seems to have followed the lines of the old, and some of the earlier sculptures were re-used for its adornment or built at random into its foundations. Thus we are able to form some criterion of the styles of the two periods of Hittite sculpture, a criterion which with due caution we can apply elsewhere, where external evidence is less assuring.

There is no doubt that a large Hittite quarter existed outside the city walls, between the south gate and the modern village of Jerablus, though but little now remains in evidence thereof. Later on, Roman villas were built here, and centuries of agriculture followed : where little more than the pavements survive of these stone-built Roman houses it is natural that the mud-brick work of the Hittites has left no trace behind. But below the railway bridge a river-wall of massive stone still holds up the bank of the Euphrates, and behind this there was probably a settlement of the poorer classes: perhaps even the bulk of the population lived here in normal times, and only moved into the city proper when danger threatened from without. In that case the walled town of the Kala'at would have been a town of temples and palaces, offices and barracks; the position of the Hittites, or of the Mushki, as a conquering minority ruling a subject people of older stock, much as in the twelfth century the Normans and their imported followers held England, would agree well with such a theory, and certainly, so far as our excavations have gone at present, we have found within the walls only Government buildings, temples, and the houses of great men or kings.

The road from the water-gate leads inland to an open square lying at the foot of the acropolis. Facing you as you come up, on the far side of the square, is what we call the Processional Wall. This wall differs from any other yet found in that its frieze of sculpture is not on the ground-level, but stands some four feet up over courses of plain and heavy masonry. The reliefs, on slabs of limestone and basalt placed alternately, had slipped from their places and lay against the wall's foot, or were embedded in the concrete foundations of the Roman buildings which overlay the silt; but all that have yet come to light have been replaced in position, and though some are missing, there are enough left to make this frieze of warriors a very imposing thing. At the rear of the line come foot-soldiers marching two by two, in front are chariots whose horses trample upon the beaten enemy, or their lords shoot down the flying with arrows; on the last slab, bringing the procession to a halt, as it were, stands the figure of the goddess, Ishtar or some kindred type, naked and holding her breasts, the symbol and the spirit of the temple to which the army brings its triumph. In the middle of the row, between the chariots and the footmen, is a slab, the largest of all, inscribed with the story of their warfare: one cannot read it as yet, but the severed hands and heads that end

CARCHEMISH: SCULPTURED SLAB AT THE FOOT OF THE LOWER PALACE STAIRCASE.

the text betray the meaning and confirm the victory.

Beyond the Ishtar slab and at right angles to the Processional Wall is a wide flight of steps that leads from the square up the hillside, which was terraced to take the lower rooms of a palace whose main quarter must have been upon the top of the mound. The stairway was lined on either side with sculptures in relief, all of basalt, and at its head was an entrance-door flanked by lions carved in the same black stone; smaller doorways to right and left gave access to the terrace chambers. It has suffered much from the ravages of time, and much too from the reckless excavations carried out here some thirty years ago: some fragments of the wall sculptures are in the British Museum to-day, others were broken by the excavators, or left exposed to be destroyed by natives, and not a single slab remains intact in its place; but, in spite of all, the broad staircase in its ruined setting is a fine example of Hittite architecture, and gives a monumental aspect to this corner of the public square. On the right of the stair's foot, balancing the Processional Wall and happily framing the stairway, stands a huge slab of basalt whereon are represented the three gods of the Hittite trinity. This sculpture must have remained exposed throughout all the periods which succeeded the fall of Carchemish; it was above ground when George Smith visited Jerablus in 1876, and it is remarkable indeed that it should have been neither shifted nor defaced.

On the south side of the square is another palace whose whole front is adorned with sculptures. Fronting the stairway we have a long series of mythological scenes, strange monsters in conflict, an archer mounted on a camel, the fever-demon, the Lord of Thunder and the Lord of Beasts, black slabs and white, whose subjects seem to stand in little relation one to another. Then the wall turns back to form a re-entrant angle, and the pictured scenes change: instead of ill-understood gods and demons we see here a row of shield-bearing warriors arrayed in tall plumed helmets, greaves and breastplates, strangely like Athenian soldiers of the fifth century B.C., who march in twos toward the palace door: the wall turns again, and at the head of their men the seven captains of the host advance, armed each in the fashion of his corps, with bow or sword, heavy spear or light javelin; the leader carries the olive branch of peace or victory. In the angle between officers and men a statue of the god Hadad stands on a lion-supported base; in strong contrast to the free and delicate carving of the reliefs is this clumsy columnar figure, a type which old convention doubtless constrained to lines so much ruder than the living art of the day: the god was found thrown down and in fragments, and we were really sorry to restore him to his pristine ugliness against the background of the Greek-looking spearmen and the exquisite captains.

Beyond the chief captain the wall turns south again, leading to the palace gate, and on it is figured

CARCHEMISH: THE ROYAL BUTTRESS.

The Hittite king and his family welcome the returning troops.

the procession which comes out thence to welcome the conquering army. A long and beautifully-cut inscription forms the corner-stone, and then we have the king and all his family. The royal children are represented twice over on the same slab: above, they march soberly in procession, but in the lower panel they have relapsed to a more congenial pastime, and are seen tossing knuckle-bones or playing whip-top, while the queen or nurse brings up the rear carrying the baby of the house—leads too its pet animal at the end of a string! It is a charmingly domestic group, and by a pretty touch of sentiment even the animal's name is duly inscribed on the stone above its head.

A group of musicians and a sphinx (both in the older Hittite style) flank a side stairway, and then the procession is renewed; the statue of the goddess is borne forth, and behind her come priests and priestesses in a long line reaching back to the doorway proper, which is flanked with further sculptures and its basalt side-posts covered with inscriptions. On the other side of the door is a great statue carved in the round, a seated god throned upon twin lions. You pass through the gateway between the guard-rooms, and an inner gate leads you to a courtyard whose walls are also sculptured in relief, and show lions and stags and huntsmen armed with bows.

Not much of the interior of this great building has been excavated as yet, but the entrance has given us interesting details which, eked out with information gained from other parts of the site, enable us to gather some idea of the original appearance of a Hittite palace. Above the carved slabs of stone the walls were carried up in mud brick, but this base material was hidden by a panelling of cedar-wood. The palace had been destroyed by fire, but the charred beams in the wall-face and the ashes heaped along the edges of the stone podium still retained something of the scent of the forests of Lebanon, and even the form of the panelling could be traced. The door-jambs were of basalt, but the framework of the folding-doors themselves was of cedar bound and studded with bronze, the bronze-shod hinges turning in sockets of polished stone. Again, in the courtyard behind the Processional Wall one can see another style of building. Here at the back of the court was a small shrine plainly built, with no carving on its limestone slabs nor other adornment than the long inscriptions cut on its door-jambs of basalt; but to atone for this simplicity the wall above was faced with glazed bricks, mostly plain blue, or with a wave-pattern of blue and yellow. But the border-bricks that framed the door and ran along above the stonework bore a design of white and yellow marguerites in slight relief against the blue ground. Thus in two buildings close together on the site we have parallels both to the House of Cedar which Hiram's workmen made at Jerusalem and to the glazed brickwork of the gates of Babylon. The influence of Mesopotamia upon Hittite (and especially late Hittite) art is obvious and expected, but the other parallel

CARCHEMISH : THE TEMPLE COURT.

The bull laver stands in the foreground, facing the shrine.

CARCHEMISH

.is more arresting. Look again at the little glazed shrine, and the Babylonian element in it will be seen to be but superficial, and a more thorough-going comparison is to be sought elsewhere. It was, as I have said, remarkably plain: inside, two columns of wood resting on stone bases supported the roof (this we find in Minoan houses and perhaps in Dagon's temple where Samson died), and the inner wall-face was probably panelled with cedar. Outside in the courtyard, directly in front of the shrine's door, stood a colossal basalt group of two oxen supporting between them a trough, which while it might have been the base of a statue, yet from the smooth wearing of its inner sides seems almost certainly to have been a basin or laver; beyond this again was an altar of burnt-offerings, a simple platform of stones and clay covered with burnt bones and ashes. The whole arrangement of courtyard and shrine is curiously reminiscent of the temple which Phœnician workmen built for Solomon, with its courts, its altar and its laver supported by oxen, its two sacred columns, and its Holy of Holies, small and unadorned. The resemblance is surely too close to be but accidental. Tyre, as we know, had been in close touch with the Hittite cities of the north, and the Phœnicians, imitative as ever, may well have found in some older Hittite shrine a model for the House of Jehovah.

The area which we have excavated up to now seems but a little patch contrasted with the Kala'at's whole extent, but to describe it in detail would be far too long a task for such a book as this: perhaps

I have indulged overmuch in detail already, seeing that the object was no more than to give the general setting of my stories of Jerablus. But the spirit of the place, of this ruin set in the wide, wind-swept, treeless land, is hard to give in words. Cross the Kala'at where the lichened Roman columns strew the grass, and walk down the earth slope to those lower levels which are Hittite ground, and you are in a strange world wherein anything might happen. To your right the Euphrates runs past in a bold curve, its brown waters eddying and leaping in their haste: the acropolis mound, scarred and seamed with trenches, rises huge and high above the river; landward the sweeping line of the walls shuts out all beyond, and gives the feeling that this is still a fenced city. You stand there on flagged pavement or cobbled court whose polished stones have not known the tread of man's feet since Carchemish went down in smoke and tumult two thousand five hundred years ago, and about you and above are the long rows of sculptured figures, gods and beasts and fighting men, and inscriptions in honour of forgotten kings; statues of old deities; wide stairways and gates, where the ashes of the doors still lie in the corners of the threshold; column-bases whose shafts were of cedar and their capitals of bronze wrought in patterns of nets and pomegranates—and the scarlet anemones push up between the stones, and the lizards sun themselves on the walls of palace or temple, and the spring wind drives the dust over the ruins of the imperial city. Very

CARCHEMISH : THE EAST WALL OF THE PROCESSIONAL ENTRY.

magnificent must Carchemish have been when its sculptures were gay with colour, when the sunlight glistened on its enamelled walls, and its sombre brick was overlaid with panels of cedar and plates of bronze; when the plumed horses rattled their chariots along its streets, and the great lords, with long embroidered robes and girdles of·black and gold, passed in and out of the carved gates of its palaces; but even now, when it lies deserted and in heaps, it has perhaps in the melancholy of its ruin found a subtler charm to offset the glory of its prime. Melancholy it is, like all ruins; but come down before the luncheon-hour is quite over, when the men are lounging at ease on the great staircase or clustered under the shadow of the Processional Wall, or when, perhaps, a couple of wandering minstrels have been enticed there, and to the sound of their shrill pipe and drum half a hundred men are circling and swaying in the palace square,—the sadness of old things is forgotten then. These idlers in their gaudy dresses, like flowers in a rock-garden, those careless brown dancers, could find no background more fitting than the tumbled stones, the steps rising like a theatre set for their out-door play; the row of sculptured chariots showing off their life against its frozen age.

HAJ W'AHID — AND OTHERS

AMONGST all the natives whom we employ at Jerablus the most striking character is Haj Wahid. An Arab from Aleppo, he is a big brawny fellow, handsome, vain-glorious, a lover of finery, honest and faithful, and a brave man for all his boasting. His besetting weakness is for strong drink, the curse of the town Arab, thanks to which he is, at forty, no longer the man he should be; but he is so far casehardened by habit that his excesses seldom force themselves upon one's notice, and as a house-servant he leaves little to be desired.

The Haj was in younger days kavass at the British Consulate in Aleppo, and considers therefore that he owes to the English an allegiance which far outweighs his duties as an Ottoman subject. The post must have suited him to perfection, for on the one hand vanity could ask no more than the magnificence of a kavass' embroidered kit, and on the other his office protected him from the results of his outrageous conduct. For it is as well to admit at once that Haj Wahid is not a model of propriety; and a lady missionary who once at Jerablus fell in love with his charming manners as a table-waiter had

not heard more than half his record before she was
refusing to be served by a man who was "a cold-
blooded murderer and worse." It was, in fact, the
exuberance of his spirits which in the end severed
his connection with the Consulate.

The Haj's house at Aleppo lay just outside the
old city walls and facing the Antaki Gate, a busy
corner where three roads converge, and the country-
folk, bringing their goods to and from the market,
jostle each other under the narrow vaulted portal.
This strategic position suggested a form of amusement of which Haj Wahid was extremely fond.
After a prolonged drinking-bout he would ensconce
himself on the flat house-roof, and thence with rifle
and revolver would hold up all the traffic of the
Gate. To try to run the gauntlet was to be made
a target for the Haj's rifle; did some camel-driver
disregard his shouts of prohibition, a bullet striking
at his feet would emphasize the order; and sometimes for a whole day at a time the gateway would
be deserted and the crowd perforce go about their
business by devious paths. As the house of the
consular kavass enjoyed what amounted to extra-
territorial rights, the town authorities were practically
helpless. A nervous policeman would edge along
beneath the house-wall, out of range from the
watcher on the roof, and call in plaintive tones,
"Dear Haj Wahid, oh, my brother, *please* let the
people come through," and the Haj would answer
with stertorous curses on the mothers and female
kin of all policemen, and would fire a few random

shots into the archway to show that the embargo still held good; and it was only when sleep brought better judgement that the public would be allowed once more to use the Antaki Gate.

Naturally a kavass whose amusements were of so violent an order was little loved by the authorities, and though the Consulate protected so long as might be a really valuable servant the end came at last. Haj Wahid was carrying on a pronounced flirtation with the daughter of a Mohammedan house, whose male members determined to put a stop to scandal. In the small hours of one night the kavass, resplendent in full uniform, had made his way out from the lady's apartments into the courtyard of her house when he was set upon by her four brothers and two others of her kinsmen. The six were armed with swords and revolvers; Haj Wahid had a revolver and the curved scimitar of his official dress. A Homeric conflict took place in the dark, and only ended when four of the assailants lay dead on the ground, one man had fallen badly wounded, and the last had fled for his life; Haj Wahid was picked up next morning in the Consulate garden, unconscious and half-dead from loss of blood, with eight wounds in his head and cuts all over him. He recovered quickly enough, but the family of his victims clamoured for vengeance; the Government took up the case with interest, and the Consul, remarking that one murder or two might have been overlooked, but four in a night was too much of a good thing, had to let the law take its course.

CARCHEMISH: THE LIVING-ROOM IN THE EXPEDITION HOUSE.

HAJ WAHID—AND OTHERS

Haj Wahid, the victim, as he still maintains, of a gross miscarriage of justice, was condemned and thrown into prison, and when at the end of three years or so he was given his liberty, the Consul felt himself unable to take back into service so turbulent a character.

When, however, the Carchemish expedition started, the Consulate could conscientiously recommend Haj Wahid as a servant, and he was engaged as cook, dragoman, and general factotum, nor has he failed to give full satisfaction. Some of his ways are peculiar. He has a passion for firearms, and is never without a revolver in his belt, even in the kitchen —in fact, should he be trying his hand at a new dish, he will sling a rifle too over his shoulder to give himself confidence for the task. A really good cook, thanks to lessons taken in the Consulate kitchen at Aleppo, he is fond of attempting novelties but is always nervous as to the result. The dish will be put down in front of me, and then without a word the Haj will take a bottle—any bottle— from the medicine cupboard and place it by the side of my plate as a sign of danger; then he will stand anxiously in the background waiting for the verdict. Should either of us make a remark in which the word "good" occurs (and we generally will strain a point to do so) there comes a fervent " El hamdu l'Illah!" ("Thank God!") from behind, and Haj Wahid slips off to the kitchen to assure Ahmed the house-boy that he is the greatest *chef* in existence.

But Haj Wahid has done more for us than cook.

He is dragoman, ready to act as interpreter, to drive a bargain, to ride out on messages (and his airs and graces on horseback are a sight to see!), or to entertain guests in our absence, and generally to protect our interests. It was during our absence in the summer of 1912 that he showed his mettle, quite in the old Aleppo vein, in what might be called the last siege of Carchemish.

I have remarked elsewhere that we started on good terms with the Germans who were stationed at Jerablus for the work of the Bagdad Railway, and amongst other things let them cart off for their new buildings such stones from our diggings as had no archæological value. The chief engineer, one Contzen, was, however, a man with whom it was hard to maintain friendly relations. He was a youngish man, tall and powerfully built, but running to fat, coarse-faced, and ill-mannered, and of that bullying type which thinks to show strength by loud shouting. He came to me towards the end of our spring season of 1912 and told me that he required large quantities of earth for making the embankment which would lead to the abutment of the bridge, and that, as rock lay close below the surface on the slope leading down to the river, earth was difficult to get; he supposed, he said, that I would have no objection to his digging away the earth mounds which lay just inside my concession and close to the line of his railway. Now these earth mounds so lightly spoken of were nothing less than the city walls of Carchemish, so I told him that I was sorry but could not allow anything of the sort. He started to argue the point, and when I remained firm tried to bluster; but I told him that, while I sympathized with his feelings, I was there for archæological purposes, and could not permit such an act of vandalism as he proposed; if he liked to take the earth from my rubbish-mounds he might do so, but the walls of Carchemish could not be touched. Fuad Bey, our Commissaire, was equally emphatic, and in the name of the Government absolutely forbade the Germans to encroach in any way upon our concession. Contzen went away in a towering rage, but I supposed that the matter was finished and gave it little further thought, though from that day all intercourse between the two European camps came to an abrupt end.

When our work closed down for the summer Haj Wahid was left in charge of the house and of the site. I went off to England, and Lawrence retired to the Lebanon to spend the hot weather in the hills. Then Contzen determined to act.

Gossiping in the village one day, Haj Wahid learnt that the Germans were recruiting local labour for the digging away of the Kala'at walls. Hardly believing the story, but feeling that it was his duty to inquire, he went up to the German camp and saw Contzen. He asked the engineer whether he really proposed to destroy the walls, and Contzen unblushingly assured him that he was about to do so with my full approval. The Haj expressed his doubts about this, and Contzen lost his temper and said that he was going to do as he pleased whether I liked it or not. Haj Wahid said that without orders from me he could not allow the work to be done; the engineer told him that he was going to start the next day, and cursing the Arab for his impertinence ordered him out of the camp.

Haj Wahid at once sent a man to the telegraph office at Birijik with a wire for Lawrence in the Lebanon, telling him of Contzen's intentions and saying that pending further orders he would hold up the work. Early the next morning, armed with a rifle and two heavy revolvers, he went out on to the Kala'at, and took up his position on the top of the threatened wall. About a hundred workmen under German supervision were laying down a light railway from the embankment to the foot of the mound; but no sooner were the rails in place and digging about to start than Haj Wahid, appearing on the sky-line, announced that he would shoot the first man who drove a pick into the walls, and would follow that up by shooting any German within range. Now, many of the Arabs collected below were our own workmen, who had not the least intention of acting against our wishes; the rest had heard of Haj Wahid's reputation and were not prepared to risk their skins for the sake of the Germans; so they retired to the far end of the line and sat down to watch events. The Germans protested, but in vain. Contzen himself appeared upon the scene and threatened, but the Haj merely levelled his rifle and warned him to keep his distance; the engineer knew that violence would only lead to trouble, so did not attempt it.

HAJ WAHID—AND OTHERS

All that day the two parties sat and watched each other, and on the next day the comedy was repeated; Haj Wahid single-handed held the walls of Carchemish, and the breaching-party remained at the far end of their railway. That night after dinner the Germans started a little revolver practice in their compound, shooting at a lighted candle; the Haj climbed up the mound again and put half-a-dozen rifle-bullets over their heads, shouting to them to stop their noise and go to bed—and the Germans obeyed. The third day passed like the first two, but Haj Wahid was getting impatient; he had received a telegram from Lawrence, now in Aleppo, telling him to hold on, but this passive way of doing things did not appeal to him. So he sent another telegram to say that the Germans seemed persistent and he therefore proposed to cut matters short by going up the next morning to their camp and killing Contzen; he ended with the hope that this course would meet with Lawrence's approval. Then he found a friend to whose care he confided the charge of his wife and his beloved son, made his will, got very drunk, and prepared to do and die on the morrow.

Meanwhile Lawrence had hurried to Aleppo and hunted up Fuad Bey and the local Minister of Public Instruction, who includes the Department of Antiquities in his official province. The Minister was horrified at the German proposals, but too nervous to forbid them on his own responsibility. Fuad Bey could hardly do anything independently of his superior officer, but sent off urgent telegrams to Constantinople, calling upon the Minister there to interfere at once: Lawrence also telegraphed, and then, having sent his wire of encouragement to Haj Wahid, perforce waited for the authorities to act. For once Constantinople moved quickly. At one and the same time Lawrence received the Haj's programme for shooting Contzen, and orders arrived for the Minister of Public Instruction to go in person to Jerablus and stop the intended desecration. Lawrence went off to find the local Director of the Bagdad Railway, whom he unearthed at a dinner-party, and asked leave to send an urgent wire to Jerablus by the Company's line. The director refused. Lawrence insisted that it was a matter of life and death, and, in answer to the question whose life was at stake, said that if the telegram was not sent our cook would shoot the chief engineer the following morning. The director laughed at the idea of an Arab cook daring to kill a German, and again refused, whereupon Lawrence said that he would ask the British Consul to come round and get the refusal in writing, together with a statement that the director assumed all responsibility for the consequences arising from it. This threat made matters look more serious, and in the end the telegram was despatched, instructing Haj Wahid to offer no further obstacle to the destruction of the walls. Lawrence did not choose to inform the German of the orders which had just been received from Stamboul, but merely arranged with him that an electric trolley should be put at the disposal of the Minister for

Public Instruction early next morning. The director, who gathered from the wording of the telegram that our opposition to the railway schemes had collapsed, made no difficulty about supplying the trolley.

Consequently, next day Haj Wahid stopped in the house, prepared to drown his disappointment in raki, and Contzen, finding no watcher on the wall, triumphantly set his men to work. Two or three feet of earth and mud-brick facing had been removed, when of a sudden the Minister (whose temper had not been improved by a long journey before breakfast) appeared on the scene, accompanied by Lawrence, and peremptorily forbade the work, upbraiding Contzen in the most direct terms for his breach of faith. The discomfiture of the attacking party was complete. The engineer had there and then to pull up his rails and dismiss his workmen, and Haj Wahid was officially congratulated on the part he had played. The fact that he had been made to look ridiculous in the eyes of the whole countryside did not increase Contzen's love for us, and from that day till the time when he was removed to another sphere there was open war between our camp and that of our neighbours.

The natives, of course, looked upon the whole thing as a contest for supremacy between Germans and English; the former had made themselves generally unpopular, and the Arabs, including those in railway employ, lost no opportunity of having a dig at the Germans. As the two camps were not a quarter of a mile apart, collisions were apt to be frequent, and at the least sign of trouble tools would be thrown down and the men—ours and theirs alike—would be clamouring to be led against the engineers. Contzen, indeed, complained that I never went to see him without having two hundred armed men at my back; and it was fortunate that, on that occasion at least, I could retort that the men were his own employees, over whom I could not be expected to have any control, so that if they did look threatening it was not my affair, as he had only to order them away. He tried to do so, and I was not surprised when they picked up stones by way of answer, and in the end I had to send them back myself to their work on the German embankment.

The following story may throw some light on the reason for the Arabs' attitude.

Our house-boy, Ahmed, was coming back one day from shopping in the village and passed a gang of natives working on the railway whose foreman owed him money. Ahmed demanded payment of the debt, the foreman refused, and a wordy wrangle followed. A German engineer on his rounds saw that work was being hindered by an outsider, but instead of just ordering him off, he called up the two soldiers of his bodyguard, seized the unfortunate Ahmed, and without any inquiry as to the origin or rights of the dispute, had him soundly flogged. Ahmed returned to the house full of woe, and as I was away Lawrence went up to the German camp to seek redress.

He found Contzen and told him that one of his

engineers had assaulted our house-servant and must accordingly apologize. Contzen pooh-poohed the whole affair; but when Lawrence showed that he was in earnest, consented to make inquiries, and sent for the engineer in question. After talking to him, he turned angrily on Lawrence. "I told you the thing was a lie," he said; "Herr X never assaulted the man at all; he merely had him flogged."

"Well, don't you call that an assault?" asked Lawrence.

"Certainly not," replied the German. "You can't use these natives without flogging them. We have men thrashed every day—it's the only method."

"We've been here longer than you have," Lawrence retorted, "and have never beaten one of our men yet, and we don't intend to let you start on them. That engineer of yours must come down with me to the village and apologize to Ahmed in public."

Contzen laughed. "Nonsense," he said, and then, turning his back, "the incident is closed."

"On the contrary," Lawrence remarked, "if you don't do as I ask I shall take the matter into my own hands."

Contzen turned round again. "Which means ——?" he asked.

"That I shall take your engineer down to the village and there flog him."

"You couldn't and you daren't do such a thing!" cried the scandalized German; but Lawrence pointed out that there was good reason for assuming that he both dared and could, and in the end the engineer had to make his apology *coram publico*, to the vast amusement of the villagers.

It will readily be believed that the slave-driving principles enunciated and practised by Contzen did not make for popularity, and one cannot blame the workmen if they were always ready to side against their German masters. Our own gang regarded them as natural enemies. Lawrence and I were sincerely anxious to avoid trouble, so that the two parties seldom came into actual collision, and when they did the result was generally more laughable than serious: but that was not our men's fault, for they were always trailing their coat-tails in front of the Germans. The most truculent of them all was Haj Wahid, and once at least he went to quite inexcusable lengths. . . .

During a winter recess, when neither Lawrence nor I was at Carchemish and the Haj was left in charge, some one told him that the Germans were finding "antikas." The truth was that in scraping the soil off the rock slope beyond the south gate for the making of their embankment they had unearthed a couple of Roman coffins rudely worked in soft limestone—things of no value or interest to us, but to the natives "antikas," and therefore ours by right of our profession. Haj Wahid went to investigate and found the labourers busily stripping the soil under the supervision of a German engineer, who was accompanied as ever by his armed Circassian guard and two Turkish soldiers. The work lay outside the Kala'at, where we had no conceivable right of interference, but that did not bother the Haj. He walked up to the German and asked what right he had to be digging up antiquities, pointing to the two coffins standing forlornly in the mud. Perhaps it was due to Haj Wahid's formidable reputation, perhaps merely from a wish to avoid trouble, that the engineer, instead of ordering him at once about his business, answered that he was perfectly within his rights, as he held permission for all that he was doing.

"Who gave you permission to find antikas?" repeated the cook.

The German, thinking that the Governor of the Province would be a name to conjure with, replied that it was the Kaimmakam of Birijik.

"The Kaimmakam of Birijik?" repeated the Haj scornfully; "but *I* am the Kaimmakam of Carchemish, and I tell you to stop."

This was too much for the German, who called to his two soldiers and ordered them to turn the intruder off the work.

"Oh, would you?" retorted Haj Wahid, and promptly knocked the engineer down, and seizing him then by the back of the neck proceeded to rub his face in the mud. "That will teach you how to behave to the Kaimmakam of Carchemish," he added, as he released his victim, and, forgetting all about the "antikas" that had caused the trouble, swaggered off to the gate of the Kala'at, while the soldiers stood undecided how to act, and the engineer was too busy getting the mud out of his mouth to issue any further orders. Strange to say, the matter, which might have been serious enough, was allowed to drop, but it did not improve our relations with the railway.

The fact was that the German engineers at Jerablus were not capable of managing natives; they neither understood nor tried to understand them, and would not even trouble to see that they received just treatment. Employing as they did large numbers of workmen—far more than we had on our excavations—they could not be expected to cultivate those personal relations that we always encouraged with our men; and it was the misfortune of the Germans rather than their fault that their employees had for them no individuality, but were mere numbers in a gang, a thing not a little galling to the independent spirit of the Arabs. But it was their fault that these employees were mercilessly exploited by sub-contractors and by foremen, and could never appeal against the injustice that was regularly meted out to them. The vast proportion of the Company's work (I speak, of course, of the section with which I am familiar) was let out to sub-contractors; these were in many cases men of straw, who ought never to have been allowed to take up a contract. Any one who could speak a little German or French and who wore European clothes was likely to get his tenders accepted without further inquiry, or to be taken on as foreman for such work as the Company was doing itself; and as most of

HAJ WAHID—AND OTHERS

the Germans knew nothing of the language or the country these fellows had a free hand. Their sole object was, with or without the collusion of the engineers, to cheat both the Company and the workmen. I know of cases where a contractor's net profits were as much as five times the sum for which his whole work could have been carried out; and the payment of the men's wages gave a seldom-neglected opportunity for sharp practice. The system was bound to lead to trouble, and though robbery from the Company was always hushed up, yet the wrongs of the workmen at last found violent expression.

A contract for digging and sifting ballast at Jerablus had been given to a penniless adventurer who had obtained more than one advance in cash for the payment of the several hundred men, mostly Kurds, employed by him. After a time the labourers' complaints grew too loud to be disregarded, and Hoffmann, Contzen's successor as chief engineer at the station, learnt to his disgust that not a penny of the sums advanced had found its way to the pockets of the workmen. Hoffmann was a well-meaning man, a great improvement on his forerunner, and he announced his intention of paying the workmen directly instead of handing the money to the contractor for further embezzlement. This was a step in the right direction, but, unluckily for himself, when pay-day came he went by the contractor's books without asking how the figures therein were obtained.

The first man who was called up to take his wages had been working for six weeks and had been promised fifteen piastres a day—a very tempting sum,—but in the books he was entered as earning something like six piastres, and from this all sorts of deductions were made, *e.g.* for bread, which the men never received, for water, which they got for themselves out of the river, and so on, with the result that Hoffmann handed over to the fellow as his due the generous sum of twenty-seven and a half piastres for his six weeks' work. The Kurd objected, and that in strong terms: Hoffmann's Circassian guard promptly answered by slashing his face with a whip, the man picked up a stone, and his example was followed by the Kurds waiting behind him, and then the Circassian shot. In a few minutes a regular fight had started, and when, attracted by the noise of firing, Lawrence and I ran up the grassy mound of the old walls, we saw a very pretty little skirmish going on just below us. The Germans held the embankment of the permanent way and a small stone hut on the near side of it: the Kurds were sheltering behind the parallel embankment of the temporary line, which ran closer to the Kala'at, and both sides were dodging up and down and exchanging shots at twenty yards' range. The workmen, being the worse armed (many were throwing stones only), had started to bolt under cover of the bank towards the river, and, making a detour, thence began to flock up from behind and join us on the hilltop: presently about three hundred Kurds and Arabs were gathered there, half of them properly armed, the rest with iron bars and stones, and all swearing vengeance on the Germans.

Lawrence and I tried to hold the mutineers in check, but it was hard work, especially as the Germans would keep on firing at them: indeed, Hoffmann's own Circassian twice shot quite deliberately at Lawrence and myself, and the range being but seventy yards we were lucky in not being hit; as it was, one of his bullets struck between my feet, and the other wounded a boy to whom Lawrence was talking. We went down to the Germans and begged them to cease fire as otherwise we could not control matters, but both they and their followers had quite lost their heads and were more anxious to assault us than to listen to us, so we had to go back again. The constant if not very effective fire of the Germans, and the wounding of a few men, with tales of others killed below, excited the Kurds to the utmost: one or two women started "keening" for the fallen and shrieked to their men folk to "kill the Christians" (I protested to one old hag who was loudest in this cry, but I was assured that it did not include Englishmen!), and if we had not been loyally supported by Haj Wahid, Hamoudi, and a few others of our own men we could never have kept the Kurds under control. We had to use force to stop would-be leaders who began charging down the slope, and others of the more violent we got rid of by making them carry the wounded off to our house, but it was two hours before the Germans had fired their last desultory shot and we could persuade the whole lot of Kurds to draw off and ourselves get back to the house to look after casualties. On the men's side one had been killed and eight wounded; on the German, bruises and cuts were the worst evil suffered, for from the time the Kurds joined us on the hill not a single shot had been fired nor one stone thrown at the Germans below. The affair, therefore, was not so serious as it might easily have been, or as reports both in Syria and in Europe painted, but it was sufficiently unpleasant, and we were devoutly thankful that it was no worse.

The Germans, however, did not easily recover from their fright. At the first alarm they had despatched a telegram to Aleppo saying that their camp was being fired on and assistance was urgently required: somehow the message got mistranslated, with the result that in the course of the evening a special train arrived bringing the Aleppo Volunteer Fire Brigade, brass helmets and all! When that mistake had been put right, two hundred troops came and were stationed in the German camp: no engineer would go outside the gates without an escort of twenty men at least, and the work of the advanced section of the Bagdad Railway came to an abrupt standstill.

In reality there was nothing much to fear from the village, as few of the Jerablus men had been involved; but the workman who was killed was a Kurd of Busrawi's *ashira*, and his whole tribe at once took up the blood-feud and announced that they would prevent by force all railway work east of the river. A commission of inquiry, headed by the Vali, was held at Jerablus, and its report was most unfavourable to the Germans, though, of course, there was no idea of interfering with the Bagdad Railway as such; but when the director put forward the Kurdish difficulty and asked the Vali to settle it, if necessary by sending troops, the answer was that the Turkish Government did not wish to quarrel with the Kurds, that the blame for their attitude rested with the Germans, and that it was for the Germans to make the peace. Unfortunately the Company could not get at Busrawi so as to come to terms with him. The Germans dared not cross the river, and the Kurds refused all communications, while the Vali prudently refused to risk acting as mediator, for he knew well that the sheikh would pay no attention to him. A week went by, during which the engineers lay low in their camp, Busrawi's armed followers patrolled the deserted line, and not a stroke of work had been done.

At last the German Consul came up to Jerablus to see us, and to the disgust of the railway people (I say it to their credit) asked me to make peace between the Company and the Kurds. I told him that I must have a free hand as to terms, and he agreed, but when he heard that my first condition was the payment of blood-money, he refused with the utmost indignation, protesting that the Germans had acted in self-defence, and that the Kurds had no legal case. I asked whether he thought he was in Berlin or Mesopotamia, and pointed out that you could only settle a tribal matter such as this by tribal custom;

and at last he saw reason and left the matter in my charge. We sent for Busrawi, who came in in no very conciliatory mood, but as he really did not want trouble and did want to get his share of the cash, he soon made it clear that to please the English he would compromise. We fixed the blood-money at £120 and arranged proper safeguards for the future, putting on to the work some of Busrawi's head-men, who should be paid by the Company and should receive all complaints from Kurdish workmen for transmission to headquarters, while Busrawi on his part accepted personal responsibility for any trouble that might arise through his followers breaking the terms. We put everything in writing and sent him off to the British Consulate, and in due course the agreement was confirmed. Busrawi kept his promise, and so far as I know (for this was in March 1914) nothing more happened to break the peace in his dominions.

In connection with this affair of the fight I owe a word of thanks to Fuad Bey. At all excavations carried on in Turkey there must be present an "Imperial Commissaire," whose duty it is to act as a spy on the honesty of the excavators and to take charge of all objects of value found by them, sending an inventory of the same to Constantinople: he is also supposed to settle differences with local landlords, workmen, etc., and generally to see that the foreigners behave themselves. In 1911 the functionaries who succeeded one another in this post were both incapable and dishonest, and Hogarth had requested that a new man be sent for the following season. In

A GROUP OF WORKMEN.

Haj Wahid, holding a revolver, stands behind the Author; Fuad Bey, Imperial Commissaire, is seated on his left, next to the village sergeant-major.

1912, therefore, we were joined by Fuad Bey. An Arab of a good Bagdad family, he had spent all his life in Constantinople and was as much a Turk as imitation could make him—indeed, he could speak only a few words of his native Arabic. He had passed through the Civil Service College at Stamboul, and had been attached as clerical A.D.C. to the Vali of Aleppo, so as to get practical experience to fit him for the post of second-class Kaimmakam, which would be his first step on the ladder of office. He was a little fellow, about 22 years old, of mean physique, pasty-faced, and faint-hearted: he was convinced that we were out to steal every "antika" we could lay hands on, and would therefore make things unpleasant for him, and like a thorough-bred city youth he looked upon Bedouins and Kurds as beasts of prey whose chief amusement was throat-slitting. He came to us, therefore, under protest, nearly wept when he found that he had to sleep under canvas on the Kala'at, swallowed with open mouth the stories of the ghosts that haunted the ruins, and would not go to bed without an armed man stretched across his tent-door.

On the other hand, he was conscientious in his work and strictly honest. He set himself to learn Arabic (for he knew no French or English), and as he talked to the men gradually lost his fear of them. He used to set traps for us by leaving small "antikas" about, until at length, when I had reproved him more than once for carelessness, he grew convinced that we really did not mean to steal the things which we had promised to hand over to the Government. Thus reassured, he threw himself into the work with enthusiasm, and became a real help to us: he took a great pride in arranging and cleaning our field museum, tried to acquire some knowledge of ancient history, and even developed views of his own on comparative dates. At the same time he improved physically, thanks to an open-air life and early hours, and took to studying local conditions with a view to a better exercise of power when he should have a province of his own. The description that I have given of Fuad Bey at his first coming is quoted almost in his own words; by 1914 he was a pleasant and a helpful companion, and as he said himself, more of a man than he had ever hoped to be.

When, in March 1914, the Commission was inquiring into the matter of the Kurdish fight, the Vali and all the rest of them came down to the house to get our version of the story. Having done this, the Vali, who perhaps would not have been sorry to see all Europeans tarred with the same brush, began asking whether we had never had trouble with our workmen. I said "No," and on his urging, "Not even in the matter of pay?" had again denied it, when Fuad Bey jumped up and interposed, "Oh yes, but there is sometimes," he said; "in fact, we had a dispute only last week." I was furious, thinking that the little man was trying to curry favour by a false charge, and the score or so of Turkish officials present smiled broadly at my discomfiture.

HAJ WAHID—AND OTHERS

"Now we shall have the truth," said the Vali, "but first, Fuad Effendi, describe the way in which wages are given out."

Fuad answered truthfully enough. "A table is put out in the courtyard," he said, "with all the money on it; Mr. Woolley has the pay-book and reads out the men's names in order, and the chawîsh, Hamoudi, stands by and calls them up, and Mr. Woolley then tells the man what is due to him, and Mr. Lawrence, who sits at the table, hands the money over."

"And where are the soldiers?"

"There never are any soldiers."

"Very wrong," commented the Vali; "the soldiers should always be there to prevent trouble. Now tell us what happened last week."

Fuad took up his tale. "Mr. Woolley called up one man, a Kurd, and said he had been working six days at nine piastres, and the man agreed, and Mr. Lawrence gave him his money."

"Ah! and *how much* did Mr. Lawrence give him?"

"Fifty-four piastres."

"But that was right!" said the Vali; "what was the difficulty?"

"Well, the man took the money, but a moment later he came back and put half of it on the table and said it was not his. Mr. Woolley asked him why, and he said that at the end of last season he took a week's wage in advance, but the work closed down after three days, so he had to pay back half of his first week's pay of this year. Mr. Woolley said last season's accounts were closed and he couldn't go back on them, and the man must take the money, and the Kurd said he would not, because he hadn't earned it, and Mr. Woolley said he could have it as baksheesh, and the man said he hadn't found anything worth paying for—and I assure your Excellence there was quite a lot of trouble about it!"

The Turks were too taken aback to laugh as I was doing at the Commissaire's little trick. At last the Vali spoke.

"Do you mean to tell me," he said, "that a *Kurd* would not take all the money he could get simply because he hadn't earned it?"

Then Fuad Bey made his point. "Your Excellence," he replied, "when I first came to Jerablus I thought, as all Turks think, that these villagers were savages and wild beasts. Since I have been here I have learnt that if you treat them properly they are quite good and honest men, and it is only when people like the Germans treat them as beasts that they behave as such." It was sententious, but it was a bold speech for Fuad to address to the Vali, and that dignitary was not a little impressed. At any rate, when he had thanked us for having kept the Kurds in check, and we had told him that the real credit lay with Haj Wahid, Hamoudi, Midai the Kurd and others, who had helped us against all their natural feelings, he sent for them all, and as they in their working clothes filed in to the sitting-room the Vali turned to his fellow-commissioners and said very quietly, "Gentlemen, you will remain standing in the presence of these men." I think that Jellal Pasha himself and the commissioners who saluted and stood silent while he thanked the despised villagers really learnt a lesson from Fuad Bey that morning.

On another occasion, too, he showed unexpected spirit. I was anxious to dig some graves of the Late Hittite Period, and as the cemetery lay outside the limits of our concession I was obliged to ask for a special permit. The authorities at Constantinople instructed the Aleppo Minister for Public Instruction to look into the matter, and he accordingly came out to visit us and see the site. Holussi Bey had always been extremely friendly, and had shown quite a keen interest in our work; on the present occasion he did not want to interfere, but evidently misliked taking any responsibility on himself, and the most we could get him to say was that he would report favourably to Constantinople. To refer things back to headquarters meant a long delay and was quite unnecessary in view of the instructions he had received, but, argue as I would, the Minister could not bring himself to give permission offhand. His reluctance was increased by the fact that part of the site where I wished to dig was occupied by a modern graveyard, and he was afraid of stirring up local religious feeling by letting the place be desecrated—though, of course, I had promised to be most careful in avoiding offence, and had already made all the local arrangements necessary. Things had indeed come to a deadlock when Fuad Bey, looking very nervous, asked me to leave the room as he wished to talk to the Mudir in private. I went out, and from the courtyard could hear voices raised in very heated dispute; when I came back the Minister looked worried and the Commissaire triumphant.

"I have discussed the matter with Fuad Effendi," said Holussi Bey, "and I will write to Constantinople saying I see no objection to the scheme; and in the meantime you may do a little work—just a little—with a few men on the far side of the site."

I thanked him, with mental reservations, but Fuad Bey made these unnecessary. "You can work wherever you please and with all the men you want," he remarked with a severe look at his superior, "and *I* will be responsible to Constantinople."

The Mudir did not even attempt a rebuke, nor insist on his conditions; we started work happily next day, and no objection was ever raised. But before he left us, Holussi Bey took me aside. "I don't know what you have done to Fuad," he said, "but he is greatly changed; he seems to be becoming quite English!"

No description of our work at Jerablus would be complete, or even fair, without a word concerning Hamoudi, our chawîsh or head foreman. Rather tall, gaunt, with a thin sandy beard cut short, long-armed and immensely powerful, he is a striking figure at all times, but if things go wrong, or if big discoveries are on hand and the work has to be pushed, then his eyes blaze, the skin is drawn tight over the

THE HEAD-MEN.

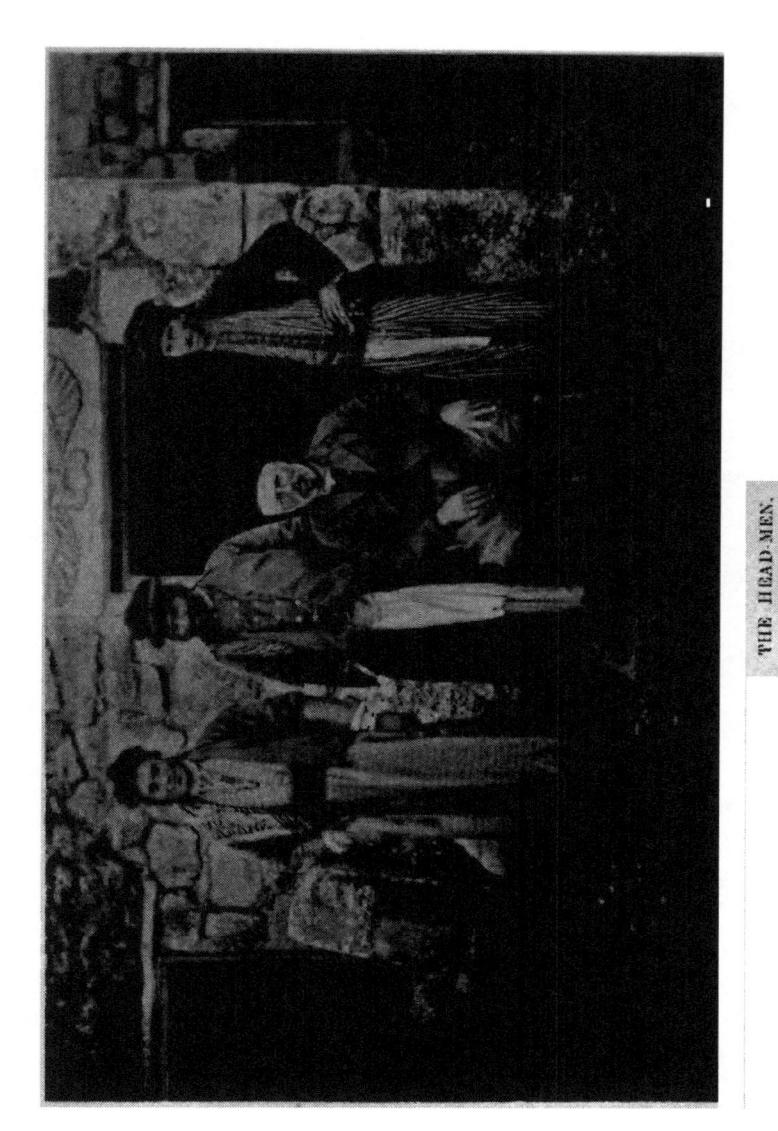

Gregori seated; behind him, from left to right, Dahûm, Abd es Sala'am, Hamoudi.

face-bones, his teeth are bared, and the man labours like a fury and looks like a devil. He affects a long-sleeved coat of sham astrakhan worn over the skirt of many colours which our men call "the Seven Kings"; his head-cloth is of purple silk and gold tissue, the "brîm" or black woollen rope that holds it in place is vastly thick and tweaked up in front to show a man of spirit and fashion; his belt is of leather and well stocked with cartridges for the inevitable revolver; his socks are European but gaudy.

Though of a most reputable stock—indeed, his written pedigree goes back to the time and to the house of the Prophet, and his father was a man of saintly life — Hamoudi has known his troubles. For five years he was an outlaw, with as many as sixty soldiers on his track, but well mounted and well armed, with friends all down the river ready to shelter him, he was never caught. His narrowest escape was once when he ventured back to Jerablus to see his wife, and some enemy betrayed his presence to the troops. It was early summer, and Hamoudi was asleep on the flat roof of his house when a summons from below woke him; looking down he saw a Turkish officer and soldiers posted all about the house. The officer summoned him to surrender. "The house is surrounded," he said; "you had better come down quietly." Hamoudi looked below. "It is as God wills," he answered, "but I am naked and in bed; let me first dress myself, that I may not be shamed, and I will come down to you." The officer agreed to the delay, glad enough, in all likelihood, to have taken so desperate a character so easily. Hamoudi whispered his instructions to his wife, and while he dressed she slipped down and, unhindered by the soldiers, who recognized her for a woman, made her way to the open pent-roof shed where was her husband's horse and unhobbled him and held him ready. A moment or two later Hamoudi hailed the officer again. "Are you ready at the door?" he asked, "for I am coming down." The officer took his stand before the door, immediately below where Hamoudi stood. The outlaw, now dressed, picked up the heavy quilted mattress on which he had been sleeping, and, holding it before him, jumped straight on to the top of the Turk. Down went the officer with all the breath knocked out of him; up jumped Hamoudi, and before the alarm could be given was at the stable and on horseback. The soldiers fired into the darkness, but a few shots fired back in defiance and a shout of derision told them that their victim had slipped through their fingers.

When in 1908 a general amnesty was declared, Hamoudi, tired of his outlawry, came back to the village and settled down to a peaceful life; but the old restless spirit is not wholly dead in him. When the work is dull, or when towards a season's end the strain of his job tells on him and he gets headachey and nervous, then he will shake himself impatiently and sigh for the freer life. "Oh, Effendim," he will say at such times, "give me a hundred pounds, so that I can leave my house to take care of itself and buy a good horse and a rifle, and I'll have done with all this! I'll shoot a man or two and take to the hills again, and, by God, I should be happier than living within walls like a cow!"

The recklessness of the man is shown by the following story.

His brother Mustapha owned a melon-patch. I fancy that a few melons had been stolen; anyhow Hamoudi was arguing that they might be, and that his brother did not take proper care of his crop. Mustapha maintained that as he himself slept in the little reed shelter amongst the vines everything was safe; Hamoudi retorted that as he *slept* there everything could be stolen—"I bet that I could steal them myself without waking you," he added, and Mustapha took up the bet. That night Hamoudi with a friend crept into the melon-patch, and while the friend collected a couple of sackfuls of fruit Hamoudi took his stand inside the shelter with a heavy wooden club, iron-spiked, balanced over his sleeping brother's head. "I was ready to hit him as soon as he woke up, but he never woke," he told me afterwards. "But, Hamoudi," I said, "if you had hit Mustapha on the head with this thing you'd have killed him!" "Possibly," he answered, "but then he had said that I could not steal his melons!"

But for all the wildness in his blood, Hamoudi is very proud of his position as chawîsh and fully alive to its responsibilities. He was appointed by Hogarth, nor could a better selection have been made, and

Hamoudi himself is never tired of telling how he rose to honour. Hogarth started work in 1911 with about a hundred men collected at random from the neighbouring villages; the first thing to be done was to weed out the stupid and the slackers, and the process of sending such about their business was started on the first day. About the third day Hamoudi was called up; he was working with a pick, and Hogarth had noticed both the energy and the obvious character of the man. But Hamoudi was horrified; he expected instant dismissal, and it was no small thing to interview Hogarth, who had already earned amongst the workmen the nickname of Azrael or the Angel of Death, thanks to the temper he showed when on the work before breakfast had exerted its mellowing influence. So Hamoudi came up with shaking knees, trying to find courage to ask that he might at least carry a basket, or else retain his pick and be given double his allowance of spade- and basket-men, anything rather than be sent off in disgrace. When he was told that he was to be foreman of the whole gang he could hardly believe his ears: he had to go off and say his prayers, " a thing I had not done for a long time "—but since that day he has shown himself fully worthy of the trust put in him.

It was decided from the outset that the chawîsh should not have any voice in the enrolment of new workmen, and I had seen too much corruption and favouritism in Egypt (where the " reis " often provides his own gang) to give any licence in this respect:

Hamoudi may report that a man is a good or a bad worker, but he cannot engage a man nor dismiss one, though in the case of trouble on the work in our absence he can send off an unruly character pending appeal to us. Only once, I think, has our chawîsh put in a really strong plea for a man on purely personal grounds, and then the circumstances were peculiar. He had asked me one day whether I wanted any fresh hands, and when I said no, dropped the subject, only to take it up again some days later, with the same result. Another week passed, and he came to me in the evening with his trouble. A distant cousin, who lived some fifty miles down river, hearing of Hamoudi's high position and supposing that the usual patronage was at his disposal, had come to Jerablus with his wife and two small children, and settling himself as a guest in his relative's house had asked to be taken on at the diggings. When Hamoudi told him that that was not in his gift the cousin thought him a liar, and stayed on; as time passed and nothing happened he decided that bribery must reinforce the claims of blood, and offered Hamoudi four pounds for the appointment. Again Hamoudi explained that he was helpless, and again the aspirant was incredulous. "I don't say that he is a good man, Effendim," said our poor chawîsh, "and I don't suppose he's worse than the others; but he has been three weeks now in my house, with his wife and children, and they eat enormously, and won't go away! It is a disgrace to me to ask a thing for my own kindred against rules—but please either take him on or get rid of him!" I need hardly say that the man was given a job, on the condition that he set up house for himself!

Not the least of Hamoudi's prerogatives is that of saluting finds; it is now a regular feature of our work that any really good discovery is celebrated with a *feu de joie* from the chawîsh's revolver. This very natural mode of expression was at first indulged in by everybody, the finder thus announcing his good luck to the rest, but now there is a ritual in such matters. As soon as anything of value turns up Hamoudi is on the spot—if possible without letting Lawrence or myself know what is forward—and he helps to clear the object, and then, when it is fairly visible, adjudges its value in cartridges. A fair-sized fragment of sculpture may be put down at one shot, a complete basalt slab with figures and inscriptions will rise to seven or eight, and so, whether we are on the work or in the house, we can by listening to Hamoudi's revolver make a very fair guess as to what he has to show us. But the object of the firing is not simply to draw our attention—it is a baksheesh to the finder, valued quite as highly as the reward in cash that luck has added to his wage, and at the same time it is, in the eyes of many of the men at least, a form of homage to the stone or to the fortune that put it in their path. The finder will grow quite pathetic over the chawîsh's judgement. "Oh, but six shots, yah chawîsh, six shots: was it not five for the chariot yonder? And here there are three sons of

Adam; by God, they deserve two rounds apiece"; and the men will count up throughout the season how many cartridges have been expended in honour of their finds. I remember one Yasin Hussein coming to me almost in tears and saying that he was leaving the work; I asked him why, and then he burst out, "Effendim, I cannot stand it; my luck is evil: this season so much has been found, there is shooting every day—now it is Hamdôsh, ping-ping-ping, now it is Mustapha Aissa, ping-ping-ping-ping, now another, but for me not one cartridge since work started. I must go, Effendim, or else you must put me where I shall find something. Honestly, I don't want the baksheesh—don't give me money for it; it is the honour of the thing—I want to hear the chawîsh shooting for me, and to have men saying afterwards, 'That is the stone of Yasin Hussein for which he had eight shots.'"

The whole thing may sound childish, as much on our part for encouraging the practice (for we keep Hamoudi in cartridges) as on the men's for caring so deeply for it; but in fact it is such things that make the work go well, and when digging at Jerablus ceases to be a great game and becomes, as in Egypt, a mere business, it will be a bad thing for the work. But as long as we have people like Haj Wahid and Hamoudi with us life is not likely to be altogether dull.

There is another way in which the high spirits of our workmen can be turned to good account. The whole gang is divided into companies of four, consisting of a pick-man, a shoveller, and two basket-men who carry the loose earth from the diggings to the light railway, which transports it clear of the work and dumps it in the river. All these are paid alike, but there is great emulation for the post of pick-man, for he has on the whole the easiest job, and also has far the best chance of finding antiquities and thereby earning baksheesh and honour. The pick-men therefore are carefully selected from the best workers in the whole gang, the spade-men are in the second grade, and the basket-carriers are, for the most part, the recruits and the boys. Most of the small objects are found by the wielder of the pick, who therefore earns most; but should a thing escape him and fall to the spade-worker the reward for it is slightly raised as an encouragement to careful work; should the basket-carrier find a thing which had been overlooked by both his seniors and was therefore in danger of being lost altogether, then the reward is more generous still. Thus all eyes are on the alert, and from the time the earth is first loosened till the moment when it is chucked down the dump-side some one is always searching it for "finds." In the case of big stones the bulk of the reward goes to the pick-man who unearths it, and the remainder is divided in proportion between the other three members of his gang. All this leads to a good-humoured rivalry between the different tools, and the nature of the soil at any moment may bring this to a head. When there is to be removed a mass of soft surface soil where "finds" are unlikely, the pick-man has an easy time; he cuts down a heap of loose earth that will keep his two baskets busy for twenty minutes, maybe, and then sits down to a cigarette and the enjoyment of seeing others work; the spade-man too has a light job filling baskets, while the carriers are run nearly off their feet. On the other hand, when the ground is hard and stony the pick cannot make progress fast enough; the carriers come up and sit on their baskets waiting for a load and the spade-man has nothing to give them. In either case Hamoudi sees his chance, and, standing on a mound with his head-rope on one side and his hands in his pockets, he will pour scorn on one side or the other. If the earth is soft and plentiful, he begs the picks to kill the basket-carriers, sons of sloth and eaters of unearned bread; if the picks are wrestling with stones and hard-set earth, he will exhort the basket-men to make the pick-fellows, greedy seekers after baksheesh, cry "pardûn."

At once the fun begins. Both sides fall to work with a frenzy, the pick-men taunt the baskets and the basket-carriers threaten the picks; the latter, if the ground is hard, will soon be pouring with sweat and writhing under the opprobrium of the waiting basket-men, while these, if soil is soft, will be racing at full speed from trench to truck, pick and spade-men shouting to them to hurry up: it is "Baskets, baskets, ho! baskets!" from the one side, and "Earth, earth, give us earth!" from the other; the excitement grows, and the noise gets louder and louder, while Hamoudi from his perch with wild gesticulations cheers on both sides alike; the men grow exhausted, and the winning side yells all the louder, demanding that the others say "pardûn." "Never!" will cry the pick-men, if they be the challenged side, "we will die, but we will not say pardûn," and they will attack the wall of earth and stone as if their lives really depended on the effort. But the baskets work too fast for them and the spade-men can find no loose soil to scrape up: then the empty baskets are hurled into the air with screams of triumph, or flung at the heads of the pick-men as they sink breathless and fagged-out to the ground. Hamoudi, as umpire, raises his hand and grants them ten minutes' rest wherein the weary gang can refresh itself with cigarettes and laughter—and a good hour's work has been done in twenty minutes! Of course this is only allowed when barren soil is to be cleared, but then, when there are no "finds" to keep up the men's interest, to let them go "fantêh," as we call it, is the quickest way of getting through a dull job and acts like a tonic on the men. You can only do it once or twice a day, for the fury of the work—or game—is too exhausting, but it is a fine system, and one of the most amusing things to watch.

The phrase "pardûn" deserves explanation. The leading man and chief landowner of Jerablus is one Salem Tuma, an ex-camel-driver who by usurious ways has amassed money and bought a good deal of real estate. While the railway station was being

"YALLAH!"

Pulling up a big stone; Hamoudi encourages the men. Behind Hamoudi are Gregori, the Greek foreman, and Fuad Bey.

built at Jerablus, the carts fetching stone from the quarry and the donkeys bringing water from the mill-stream used to pass this way and that over plough-land belonging to Salem Tuma and did no little harm to his crops. He explained to the Germans that this damage would have to be taken into account when his claims for compensation were settled, but the chief engineer informed him that they would pay for the ground on which the station stood and not a penny more. One morning, therefore, Salem went out with his brother and nephew and servants, all mounted and armed, and by force prevented any one from trespassing on his fields. The Germans did not like to use violence, and, while they would not altogether recant, did undertake not to use the field-paths until some agreement had been made—in other words, they stopped the building of the station.

Highly elated at having thus held up the Bagdad Railway, Salem returned to the village and there fell in with a cart-load of mud bricks being driven to the Kala'at—it was part of a lot which I had ordered for some building we were doing. He told the driver to throw the bricks out on the roadway, and when the man said they were my bricks, exclaimed that he would have no foreigners working in the village, and calling up his men he had the bricks tilted out and proceeded to smash them up with his own hands.

The news of this outrage reached me at breakfast-time, so I sent down to the works to say that after the meal I wanted all men who were not Salem Tuma's tenants to come up to the house. The story had been published on the diggings, however, and when I came out after breakfast I found the whole gang there, with pick-handles and revolvers, anxious for fun. With some difficulty I sent back those over whom the landowner had any hold, and with sixty or seventy men formed in fours and headed by Haj Wahid and Hamoudi we marched up to the village.

Tuma's house is a two-story building of stone, with an enclosed courtyard and a single-storied annexe whose flat roof serves as a balcony; on this balcony, overlooking the village square, Tuma and his brother were enjoying their morning coffee and their recent triumph.

Coming up from behind, I put twenty men to guard the back door and went with the rest round to the front. Tuma's gang thought it better to lie low when we entered the courtyard, but his nephew came down the balcony steps brandishing a revolver and screaming to us to clear out; he had to be knocked on the head to prevent violence. Lawrence and I, with Hamoudi and Haj Wahid, walked upstairs and found Salem and his brother in a state of abject fright. The little square below was now crowded with villagers, and the general excitement had brought up the soldiers too; one of these caught hold of one of my men and asked him what he was up to. "English work," replied the Arab, shaking his pick-handle, and the soldier said no more but joined the audience.

Salem meanwhile was giving himself away by protesting that he hadn't known the bricks were mine. I had the carter handy as a witness, so told him that he was a liar, and gave him the choice of making a public apology or being put into the village spring, which was deep and less like a spring than a well. As Haj Wahid had already started making feints over the poor man's head with a club, there was no delay. White-faced and quivering, the two fat brothers dashed to the edge of the balcony and began a shrill duet of recantation: they had not known the bricks were English bricks, they loved the English more than they loved each other, they were only too pleased that the English should make bricks, and hoped they'd make lots more. "Dakhilak," they screamed, and because they knew a few words of Syrian French, "Pardûn!"

Now "dakhilak," though the town Arab may use it lightly enough, is the strongest phrase a Bedouin knows, and it must be a matter almost of life and death before his honour will let him thus beseech another by the bowels of his mercy; to the village audience, therefore, the brothers Tuma had reached the depth of known humiliation when that appeal was made, and when hard on its heels there came the unknown word "pardûn," they could only conclude that this was something more degrading still. The crowd broke into howls of mockery: "He has said dakhilak!" "'Pardûn,' Salem Tuma says 'pardûn,'"—in a minute the simple thing had become a reproach and a byword.

We left the disconsolate pair in peace, refusing

the coffee of a formal reconciliation, but months later in quite far-off villages one boy would challenge another to a wrestle with the threat, "I'll make you say 'pardûn' like Salem Tuma," and for Jerablus the phrase has become a household proverb. Tuma himself, visiting us some time later, referred sadly to the day of his disgrace: "If I had known what 'pardûn' meant," he said, "I would have gone down into the spring before I used it. It was better to die."

This then is the reason why when they go "fantêh" our men will work till they drop, and even then refuse to voice the formula of defeat.

But though there are times when the work can be speeded up in this way, when it does not matter that the baskets are flying through the air, the men blind with sweat, and the decauville cars swinging nearly off the rails as they race each other to and from the dump-heaps, yet, on the other hand, when finds are probable, there are no more careful diggers than these Arabs. Even the Egyptian, skilful as he is with his "touriya," is not more delicate of touch than a pick-man after two seasons' practice. As soon as his sense of touch tells him that a stone which he has reached with his point below the soil but has not yet seen is a large block or one bedded in a wall, he sets to work as gingerly as though he were unearthing buried glass; then if things look promising the pickaxe is exchanged for the knife, and with Hamoudi hovering about like an anxious hen, or sometimes ousting the workman to do the job himself, the object is cleared without the possibility of damage. Again, to find and follow a mud-brick wall buried deep in soil which is itself composed of mud-bricks, loose or fallen in masses, is no easy task, especially as the wall-face is usually plastered with mud, and this plastering must remain, so far as may be, intact. The digger will cut along, trying to keep the side of his trench an inch or so away from the wall-face; then as the earth dries he will retrace his steps, and with the blunt end of his pick or with a knife dislodge the film of soil that adheres loosely to the brick-work and so expose the true surface. The men soon learn to take a pride in their skill in following the line as closely as can be without cutting into the wall itself and then in baring the undamaged face. The wall and the brick debris surrounding it are sometimes so hard to distinguish that the work has to stand over for a few days until the weathering of the bricks shows which is really wall and which but fallen wall-material, and great is the workman's joy then if he prove to have been right where I was undecided. Perhaps the greatest test of the men's skill was when we dug a late Hittite cemetery on the hillside beyond the mill-stream. Tomb-digging was new to them, and as the graves had merely been cut down deep into the soil, the urns and offerings laid at the bottom of the pit, and the earth tumbled back immediately upon them, it needed delicate handling to lay all bare for the photographer without breaking or moving from their place the fragile bowls and vases, the clay dolls and toy horsemen, and all the tomb-furniture embedded in the clinging soil. It was far more difficult work than, for instance, the clearing of prehistoric graves in Egypt, where the filling is but of sand or dry powdered brick that falls away of itself and leaves the objects free and clean; here knives had to be employed all the time, and then, as the earth dried, brushes and bellows for the final work. I gave Hamoudi a few practical lessons with the first graves, and thereafter he coached the men until they could look after themselves—though our chawîsh always gave the finishing touches before the camera was brought; and certainly the photographs we got of that graveyard are as good as any that I have seen from Egypt—and many of these photographs were taken and the plates developed by Dahûm, a village boy trained in the camp and turned out at the end of two months to work virtually "on his own."

The digging of these graves was a very pleasant interlude, and incidentally showed how important it is to have one's men well-disposed. I have mentioned elsewhere that the authorities boggled a good deal at granting permission for the work because part of the ancient cemetery was overlaid by modern burials, and the sanctity of a Moslem cemetery is far more inviolable than that of a Christian churchyard. I promised to respect every possible prejudice, and therefore started on the far fringe of the ancient graves and worked forwards toward the forbidden ground. But as we drew nearer to this the old tombs were found to be richer and more numerous, and the men's interest—and their baksheesh accounts—grew in proportion. Now the old graves were dug some six or seven feet down, deeper than the modern villager thinks necessary for his dead, and one morning, coming up rather late from breakfast, I was horrified to see one of the gangs on the very edge of the modern cemetery, and the pick-man, hot on the scent of a Hittite burial, burrowing right under a modern grave, whose stone lining hung out above his head. The rest of the gang stopped work and grinned broadly as I called the man out and told him pretty forcibly that this sort of thing couldn't be allowed, I would not have the Moslem graves disturbed. The worker looked sheepish and the rest began to laugh out loud, and then Hamoudi intervened. "It is really all right, Effendim," he urged, "that's his own grandfather!" I let him finish what he was doing, but would not repeat the experiment, and the village cemetery suffered no further desecration. I think that the men were rather relieved at being stopped, though they professed their willingness to dig up the whole place; but they added that if any one other than the English had worked even near their people's graves they would have made him pay dearly for it, and I know of more than one instance to prove the genuineness of the threat.

One of the curses of the digger in Egypt is the wandering antiquity-dealer, who will hang about in the neighbourhood and buy from your workmen anything that they may steal from the excavations. Only once has one of these gentry turned up at

Jerablus, and then the men were so furious at the insult to their loyalty that they were all literally out for his blood, and the tempter had to lie hidden until he could take the train back to Aleppo. They are not less keen to prevent any outsider from taking photographs, and if I do give permission to a visitor to snapshot one or two points of general interest, either Lawrence or myself must always go with him or there will surely be trouble; indeed on one occasion, when I was delayed on the way down and reached the field a little behind my guest, I found him looking very bewildered and not a little alarmed, with Hamoudi holding his camera and half-a-dozen workmen with revolvers blocking the view of his proposed "subject." On another occasion it was only a timely disappearance that saved a Turkish Major-General from being thrown into the Euphrates because one of his staff had tried to photograph a bas-relief against the orders of the Arab on guard; luckily the men were at work some way off on the cemetery site, and by the time the alarm had been given and they were streaming pell-mell across the intervening fields the General had effected a strategic retirement from the Kala'at.

Such are our Arab workmen: loyal and good-tempered, honest, hard working,—provided that you humour them and do not press unduly or out of season, for they are not your slaves but your fellow-workers,—and careful when care is needed. They love a joke, and I keep one old grey-beard on the digging, not for the work he does, for one condition

HAJ WAHID—AND OTHERS

of his service is that he has the smallest basket, but because he is a butt whose temper never fails him, and the owner of a scurrilous wit; he is allowed something of the licence of a court-jester even at our expense, and any little friction or discontent can be dispelled by putting old Shemali to the fore. Complaints that from others might be serious become in his mouth an absurdity at which even his sympathizers are fain to laugh; a dull stretch of work is relieved by making him the martyr on whom the worst of it is laid. "And this to me who might be your grandfather," he said once to me in reproachful terms, "and, God knows, perhaps I am, for I was wild enough!" The whole gang shrieked with joy, and the biggest stones were selected for his load; the rest buckled to at full speed so as to drive him the harder, and the thankless job was run through as a game. It is a rowing maxim that you should always have a butt in the eight: it is just as important to have a jester in an Arab working gang.

These Bedouin are clever too. There is Dahûm, our photographer: he started as a water-boy when he was about sixteen, and could neither read nor write; he could count up to ten, thanks to his fingers, but if he wanted to go beyond that he had to take his shoes off and start on his toes. Lawrence encouraged him to read, and he picked up that quickly enough from the village hoja; then he was taught English numerals, so as to assist in measuring-work and to read off the figures on the tape, and in a week he was well up in the hundreds and could multiply and divide in English. He was put to photography, could develop a plate at the end of three weeks, and very soon could take a photograph by himself, judging his own exposure, focus, and everything. I do not think that an English village boy would have made quicker progress.

Dahûm's name, by the way, is curious; a nickname really, it sounded to me quite un-Arabic when I first heard it, so I asked Lawrence to find out what it was. It appeared that his mother had given him the nickname because when he was born he was a very black baby, and "Dahûm" meant a dark night when there was no moon. Then I saw it. Dahûm, the moonless dark, was Tehôm, the "darkness" that was on the face of the waters before creation, the Tiamit or Chaos-goddess of Babylonian theology, and here the name, with something of its meaning, had survived to our day. It is perhaps not for nothing that Dahûm's family claims to have lived, not in the modern village, but on the Kala'at, deserted less than a century ago, "always and always," saying that they are "the Kala'at folk" whereas most of the rest of the Jerablus people are newcomers. They are Arabs now, they say, because the rest are; but before that they were Turks, Greeks, or what not (though always Moslem!), according to the Government in power; and certainly in Dahûm's face there is little of the Arab, and something at least of those rather heavy and fleshy captains who head the sculptured procession at the portal of our Hittite palace.

Hamoudi and Dahûm are great travellers, for they

have been to Beirut, taken ship thence for Alexandria, and have visited England, and Dahûm went with us too for a journey through Turkish Sinai from Beersheba to Akaba. But they have not been sophisticated by their wanderings, and even the older man is still the unspoiled and contented outlaw that he was before he made the acquaintance of great cities. Once when we were at Beirut H.M.S. *Black Prince* was lying off the port (she has had her great day now and done her work, and with her gallant crew lies under the waters of the North Sea), and we took the two Arabs on board. They had heard in the town wondrous tales of this the first warship they had seen, and how two shells from her great turret-guns would lay all Beirut level with the dust, so their delight went beyond all bounds when it transpired that firing practice was just over and they were allowed to watch the handling of the guns. They were taken into a turret, and through the casemate they saw the town. Both exclaimed at once, "Oh, *do* shoot at the town, just two shots, at this end of it and at that!" The officer in charge of the party expostulated. "Good heavens, no!" he exclaimed, "why, it would knock half the place to bits!" "Yes," urged Hamoudi, "but it's a bad town—and it would be *such* fun!" and the one blot on their happiness was that when they left the ship Beirut still stood untouched by shot and shell.

To go to England was a treat undreamed of, taken in the spirit of schoolboys, but with a joy made somewhat tremulous by the dire forebodings of their friends that they would never come back. Even Hamoudi was rather deliciously uncertain about the truth of our solemn yarn telling how natives were enticed to England and then turned into tinned meat, and he admitted afterwards that his coming was a supreme act of faith in ourselves. But though they had their fill of wonders abroad it was to them but an excursion from which they came back gladly to their village life: they saw the convenience of much that was Western (Hamoudi particularly wanted to pocket and take home with him an ordinary bath-tap, so as to have hot water always handy without the bother of lighting fires!), but the meal of herbs at Jerablus was, as a permanent thing, far to be preferred to the stalled ox of England. That is a thing we have always tried to teach them, that what is good for the one is not necessarily good for the other, and that the Arab who throws over his own civilization to ape the European is a worse man thereby. At first our workmen did not quite see why, if one of them came down wearing a shoddy waistcoat or with European boots instead of native red shoes, he should straightway be sent off the work in disgrace: then they found out that we wanted them to remain themselves and to respect themselves as such, and they had the wit to apply the lesson to other things besides clothes, and to weigh anything European in the balance of their own nationality, their habits, their prejudices, and their religion, before they would allow of its adoption. There is no reason why these people should not travel by rail or improve their ways of agriculture and have medicines for their sick, but may a kindly Providence long postpone the day when the officious West shall impose on them the evils of an alien civilization and to widen its commerce or to gratify the impertinence of its missionary spirit shall make hybrid degenerates of the gay, self-reliant Arabs who were our working gang at Jerablus.

THE KAIMMAKAM OF BIRIJIK

ABOUT five-and-twenty miles upstream from Jerablus there is the little town of Birijik, the seat of a Kaimmakam and the headquarters of the sub-province within which lies the site of Carchemish. It stands on the left bank of the Euphrates, a huddle of small houses, a khan or two, a rather squalid little bazaar, which forms the main street running parallel to the river, and at the north end of this the Serai or Government House built out over the water beneath the shadow of the Castle cliff. It is the castle that redeems Birijik from the utterly commonplace. A great bluff of rock rises abruptly from the river and is crowned by a fine twelfth-century stronghold which the Atabegs built here to keep in check the crusading country of Edessa. Still almost intact— no thanks to the Turks, for in 1909 the local government decided on its destruction and was only stopped by the interference of English travellers —the old fort mercifully dwarfs the main buildings of the town below. Just opposite to the castle the road from Aleppo runs down to the western bank of the Euphrates, where the ferry is, and the great clumsy punts, high-prowed and level-sterned, wait to

THE KAIMMAKAM OF BIRIJIK 147

take carriages and all across the water; it is a passage of some four hundred yards, could they but make it direct, but the swift current bears them far down on a transverse course to land at the town's lower end, and thence they must be towed up to the rock's foot again, and so zigzag this way across and that at the river's mercy.

Standing where the road ends on the western bank one has the finest view of the castle as it towers up clear above Birijik, its massive outer walls of pink and honey-coloured limestone melting almost imperceptibly into the cliff-face from which they rise, its battlements outlined sharp against the sky, and its mellow tones reflected in broken patches of colour by the hurrying stream. And if it be springtime or summer when you come down to the ferry, you will see too from here the one other thing which gives to Birijik a character of its own. Half-way up from the water to the foundation of the castle walls there runs across the rock's face a broad horizontal ledge which is crowded with ragged nests, and perched along it or flying in the air about are hundreds of large black birds of a sort unknown in any other part of Syria. This bird, a variety of the Glossy Ibis, winters in the Sudan, and yearly in the spring a great flock migrates northward from the Nile Valley up through Palestine to Birijik, where from time immemorial they have made their home on the castle rock. In no other place along the river will you find a single nest of them; as far down as Jerablus the birds will come to feed, and you may see them wading in the shallows or flying low over the water, their jet-black plumage and curious slender crests making them easy to identify, but at sunset they all fly back to the one small spot which some freak of instinct and the habit of centuries has taught them to regard as their sole breeding-place.

When it was that the first northward-flighting ibis chose Birijik for the Mecca of his kind no one can say: but that the pilgrimage is of ancient date chance has preserved proof tangible enough. While we were building our house at Jerablus the villagers informed us that in a field three-quarters of a mile away they had come on a decorated pavement: we went to the spot and found that they had in fact unearthed a large piece of a fine mosaic floor of about the fifth century A.D. As it was quite certain that it would soon be destroyed if exposed to the weather we obtained permission to remove it, and ultimately relaid the whole as the floor of our sitting-room. The mosaic, which is well executed in moderately-sized tesserae of about eight different colours, measures some 24 feet by 12 and is divided into two main panels surrounded by a decorative border. The lower panel represents an orange tree flanked by ducks and gazelles; in the upper is a vase from which springs a great formal vine whose symmetric branches are crowded with all sorts of birds, peacocks, pheasants, and smaller fowl; near the top of the vine a life-like portrait of the Glossy Ibis bears witness that as far back as Roman days the visits of this capricious immigrant had won attention and deserved a record.

A FIFTH-CENTURY MOSAIC.

Naturally, then, a legend has grown up around the " Birijikli bird." The villagers thereabouts will tell you—and though they have not seen the ceremony they have no doubt of its occurrence—that the birds arrive on a fixed date every year, and on this day the Kaimmakam of Birijik, the Mufti, the Cadi, and the other dignitaries of the town go out in solemn procession along the river-bank south of the outlying houses and there await the arrival of their visitors. At last, far away to the south, beyond the river, they see the solitary fore-runner of the flock. Weary with his long flight the bird sinks lower and lower as he nears the home rock, rises again in a last effort to cross the river, but before ever he can win to the far bank falls exhausted and is drowned. Then a second bird comes into view, and then a third, which also have outdistanced the main body of their friends. The foremost of these, with fast-failing wings, struggles to the eastern bank, and there sinks spent but in safety at the water's edge: the other flies unfalteringly and straight across the Euphrates to the group of Turks and alights in the outstretched arms of the Kaimmakam. This, if all falls out by rule, is a sign no less sure than that of the Easter dove at Florence that the year's crops will be good and that God's blessing is on the flocks and herds; with great joy, therefore, the Turks return to the Serai, where the Kaimmakam gives food and drink to the tired harbinger of increase, and then sets it free to rejoin its fellow-pilgrims, who have in the meantime arrived and reclaimed possession of their nesting-place in the town's acropolis.

The official who in 1912 was Kaimmakam of Birijik was by no means worthy of the poetic rôle assigned to him by legend. An elderly man with grey hair and pointed beard, sly eyes, and flabby figure, ignorant and hardly more than literate, he was a fair representative of that bad type of minor official who, favoured of Abdul Hamid in older days, had on his fall espoused the cause of the Young Turks for what could be made out of it. Governing a fair-sized province wherein there were few strong enough to appeal against his powers, and owning in all civil matters but a loose allegiance to the vilayet of Aleppo, he had an ideal field for that profitable corruption which to his like is the only use of office. Unfortunately Jerablus lay within this worthy's jurisdiction, and from the very outset he and I came to loggerheads.

In 1911 Hogarth, with Campbell Thompson and Lawrence as his assistants, had started excavating at Carchemish, and it was the good result of his experimental season that induced the British Museum to undertake a prolonged campaign there. I had been asked to take charge of the work, and as in the winter of 1911–12 I was busy in Egypt I sent Lawrence up ahead of me to Jerablus to get things in order for the new season and to start building a permanent house for us. On meeting Lawrence in Aleppo at the end of February I was rather annoyed to find that matters had not gone smoothly.

He had been to Jerablus, where of course he was well known, but had been unable to start building. At the close of the former season it had been requested that a guard be put upon the site to prevent plundering and to see that no unauthorized work was done: the Kaimmakam had received orders to that effect, and a corporal with ten men had been posted in the village. When Lawrence arrived, the corporal, on the strength of his orders, had prevented the building of the house, and even the knowledge that Lawrence was a member of the expedition had not availed to get this prohibition modified in his favour: consequently, pending my arrival, nothing could be done.

It was a Sunday afternoon when Lawrence and I, travelling in wagons then, for the railway was yet to come, reached Jerablus and pitched our camp within the earthen walls of Carchemish. Eager candidates for work had flocked to meet us, but I put these off till the morning, and sent to the village for the onbashi, the corporal in charge of the guard. That N.C.O. turned up duly and was polite enough, but when I said that I proposed to begin digging at once, he demurred: he knew that I was duly authorized, but he was a soldier and had his orders, which he must obey: would I therefore send a note to Birijik, whereupon, of course, sanction would be given without delay. The man was quite in the right, so I wrote a letter to the Kaimmakam notifying him of my arrival, expressing my pleasure at the efficient way in which the site had been guarded, and asking him to instruct his N.C.O. to give me full liberty of action for my work. The letter was taken at once to Birijik by a mounted soldier of the guard, and next morning, anticipating no difficulty (for I was new to Turkish methods), I enrolled a gang of a hundred and twenty workmen and told them that digging would start on Wednesday. In the evening came the Kaimmakam's reply. It was written, not to me but to the onbashi, in Turkish, and was to the effect that the Kaimmakam neither knew who I was nor cared to know, and that I was not to be allowed to touch a stone at Jerablus.

This was a nasty shock. Prudently or imprudently, I had engaged my gang, and to put off the digging now not only meant a loss of time but would destroy the men's confidence and respect — an important thing in a country none too civilized. The only thing to do was to act at once and to see the Kaimmakam in person:—after all, I felt, it was a misunderstanding which a few minutes' talk would clear away. So early on Tuesday morning Lawrence and I, accompanied by our cook and major-domo, Haj Wahid, who was to act as interpreter should Turkish be required, took horse and set off on the long ride to Birijik.

We crossed the ferry and put up our horses at a khan behind the town, and then, after a hurried lunch (for breakfast had been early), we sought the Serai. The building forms a quadrangle enclosing a courtyard, far from clean, where a score of soldiers

THE KAIMMAKAM OF BIRIJIK 153

lounged: there was a guard-room on the ground floor, and a jail through whose gratings there peered out on us a few poor victims of Turkish justice. From the courtyard a somewhat rickety wooden staircase gave access to a broad balcony running round the upper story, where were the court-house and the various offices of the Government. We went upstairs, and having ascertained that the Kaimmakam was in his room and disengaged, I sent in my card; we waited for some little while and then sent in again, but again no answer was vouchsafed, so, telling the others to follow, I brushed past the guard and walked into the office. The Governor was seated at his desk doing nothing: he looked up, surprised by our entry, but did not ask us to sit down, so Lawrence and I made ourselves comfortable on the divan that ran along the wall close to his chair, and Haj Wahid stood by the door. At the start Haj Wahid had to act as interpreter, for the Turk knew only a few words of French, and, though he could speak Arabic, began by pretending he could not: it was only when the interview grew more exciting that he and I both dropped into Arabic and dispensed with the third person.

I introduced myself politely, and after thanking him again for the care taken of our site, explained that there had been a misunderstanding about our identity, and asked him to issue orders to his soldiers for the work to start. He answered bluntly that he would give no orders of the kind, as we had no right to the place.

"Oh yes, but I have," said I; "here is the firman from Constantinople granting permission"; and I handed it to him.

He looked at it for some time, then said, "Precisely: this is all in order, but it is made out in the name of Mr. Hogarth, whom I know, whereas your name, you tell me, is Woolley."

Now this was the weak point in my armour, for although the authorities at Constantinople had been officially informed that I was to take Hogarth's place, and had raised no objection, yet the Turkish law distinctly states that permits for excavation are non-transferable, and no written correction had been made on the papers in my possession. So I determined to avoid the issue, and agreeing that the permit was made out in Hogarth's name I pointed out that I was acting as his wakīl or representative.

"And how can you prove that?" demanded the Kaimmakam, pressing on the false scent.

"Easily," said I; "here is a letter from Mr. Hogarth authorizing me to act in his name, and here is an official communication from the British Museum, which, as you probably know, is a department of the the British Government, directing me to take Mr. Hogarth's place at Jerablus," and I handed him these two documents also.

He looked at them, then "What language are these in?" he asked.

"English," said I.

"Ah," he replied, "I do not understand English."

THE KAIMMAKAM OF BIRIJIK 155

"Well, that is simple enough," I retorted. "You have a French-speaking interpreter here; call him in and I will translate the documents into French, and he can put them into Turkish."

"I should not trust such a translation," said the Kaimmakam; "and until the British Museum issues this order in Turkish I shall pay no attention to it."

In vain I pointed out that this was absurd: the Governor refused to listen to reason in any form, and matters seemed to have reached a deadlock. So I shifted the ground again, and abandoned argument for insistence. I told him that I had been sent to do a certain piece of work, that my papers were in order, and that I could not agree to any delay: I had already engaged my workmen, and I wished to start operations the following morning.

"It is impossible," said the Kaimmakam, and ostentatiously turned over some papers on his desk to show that the interview was at an end.

"But I *shall* start to-morrow," I urged.

"I have forbidden it," said the Kaimmakam, "and I shall give further orders to the soldiers to stop you."

"You have only ten men at Jerablus," I replied, "and I have a hundred and twenty who want to work: I shall start to-morrow."

"If necessary I shall send more from here," he retorted, "but it will not be necessary."

I was getting annoyed by now. "If you send all you've got," I told him, "I shall still outnumber you, and my men are just as well armed. I only hope that you will come, at the head of your soldiers, and I shall have great pleasure in shooting you first:—for I shall certainly start to-morrow."

"This is nonsense," said he. "You would not dare to shoot at the soldiers: and you shall *not* do any work."

The position was a difficult one. I felt that the whole future of our diggings depended on the result of this interview, and that it was worth risking a lot to get success: if I gave in now, a fresh permit would certainly not be forthcoming that season, and we should have lost all caste with the natives: really to use force was of course out of the question—but would a Turk be sure of that? I looked once more at the Kaimmakam, who, with a cold shoulder turned towards us, was again fidgeting with his papers, and I made up my mind that he was not a man who would call a bluff. Taking my revolver out of its holster I got up and walking to the side of his chair put the muzzle against his left ear. "On the contrary," I said, "I shall shoot you here and now unless you give me permission to start work to-morrow." The Turk absolutely collapsed. He leant back in his chair, his hands flat on the desk before him, and tried to turn his head towards me, while his lips twisted into a wintry smile.

"Certainly," he said. "I see no reason why you should not start to-morrow."

"Will you write the order to the onbashi?"

"But with the greatest pleasure; and I will send it down by a special messenger to-night."

THE KAIMMAKAM OF BIRIJIK 157

"No, you won't," I said. "You'll write it here and now, and I'll take it down myself."

The revolver was still touching his head, and he felt that it was useless to try any further trick, so pulling a piece of paper towards him he wrote something in Turkish and handed it to me. "That is what you want," said he. "Perhaps," I replied, "but I'm not certain of the translation. Please send for the interpreter, who will put it into French for me." I sat down then, still keeping the gun handy, and the interpreter duly came and the order was found to be correct. The Kaimmakam's manner had completely changed: he pressed cigarettes on us, sent for coffee, and was full of amiable small-talk, but we soon tired of his forced civility, and cut short our visit on the plea of the long cross-country ride before us. Indeed it was dark before our weary steeds drew near to the Kala'at, and we saw the glimmering outlines of the lighted tents surrounded by a crowd of anxious workmen. Then Haj Wahid spurred his horse on ahead, and long before he reached the camp, crack! crack! his revolver firing in the air announced the news of our success. In a moment there was pandemonium: a hundred men were blazing away all the cartridges they had, and we rode in through a lane of dancing Arabs, shouting and shooting in honour of the victory, which Haj Wahid's trumpet voice was declaiming with more than Oriental imagery. It was a good beginning for our work, but if I went to bed that night tired out it was less by my fifty miles' ride than by the strain of the few minutes in which I had staked so much on a guess.

I hoped, and half believed, that our troubles with the Kaimmakam were over, for the Turk is nearly always ready to accept the *fait accompli*, however keenly he may have resisted its process: but this Turk was made of sterner—or of greedier—stuff. He had hoped, so I was told, for a substantial bribe, and though no money had changed hands and yet our work was in full swing, the hope was not dead in him and he but bided his time. But the second act in the comedy requires a prologue.

It was just about forty years ago—to be precise, in 1878—that the British Museum first started excavations at Carchemish. In those days no law had been passed forbidding the export of antiquities from Turkey, and the scientific side of field archæology had not been developed: one dug for plunder wherewith to stock Museum galleries, and was interested in nothing more than that. The monuments standing above ground at Jerablus had attracted the attention of George Smith, the father of Mesopotamian archæology, and the British Museum was induced to undertake work on the site. But, when it was simply a question of uncovering and carting away antiquities, the presence of an archæologist was not held necessary. The job was first offered to Rassam, Sir Henry Layard's assistant at Nineveh, and when he refused, the British Consul was directed to send a dragoman to carry out the work. It is not to be wondered

THE KAIMMAKAM OF BIRIJIK

at that this worthy person did more harm than good; a few broken statues and slabs covered with reliefs and inscriptions in Hittite hieroglyphs found their way to London, but fragments of these very pieces remained *in situ* undiscovered, or were thrown into the rubbish-heaps, trenches were driven through standing walls, parts of the great palace stairway were pulled up, and sculptures not deemed worthy of removal were left exposed upon the ground to be cut up into mill-stones or mutilated by idle villagers. We can only be thankful that the dragoman, liking little his surroundings or his work, reported adversely on the latter's prospects, and after a short time left the Kala'at again in peace.

But before this abortive digging started it had seemed good to the authorities to secure some such title to the site as would give them a claim to the treasures it might hide, so the Consul himself had gone up from Aleppo to negotiate for the purchase of the ground. The Arabs who once squatted on the ruins of Carchemish had, two generations earlier, left their homes there to build a new village—the modern Jerablus—outside the walls, and the deserted Kala'at or fort had become the common grazing ground of the village flocks. It was then that the Turkish Government undertook for the first time a registry of landed property in the Empire, and the Commissioners came in due course to Jerablus. As registration connoted land-tax, many of the country folk were none too eager to pose as landlords, but one man, more far-sighted than the rest, was quick to step forward and claim the whole of the Kala'at as his ancestral birthright. He was the wealthiest of the village folk, so witnesses to his title were easy to find, and without more ado the site of Carchemish was registered on the imperial rolls as the property of Ali Agha. It was to Ali, therefore, that the British Consul made his offer of purchase. But though the land had little value, and was indeed still regarded as common to the village, the owner refused to sell: he had no objection to the diggings, but he would not part with an inch of his property nor even with a part interest in it. The Consul retired to Aleppo *rebus infectis.*

Shortly after this some soldiers appeared at Jerablus, arrested Ali Agha, and carried him off to Aleppo, where he was flung into the common prison. Now unless money or influence could be brought to bear, imprisonment in Aleppo generally ended in one way: trial was problematical at the best, disease was endemic, and the only food prisoners got was what their friends or some charitable stranger might be disposed to bring. So in his sorry plight Ali bethought him of that all-powerful British Consul who had been his guest at Jerablus. A letter sent to the Consulate soon brought on the scene that dignitary himself, who sympathized heartily with his former host, was assured of his innocence, indeed of his ignorance of any charge against him, and promised to plead his cause with the powers that were. Ali Agha was profuse in gratitude. The Consul then remarked that when he had last seen his friend in happier days there had been some question of the purchase of a piece of land. The prisoner was horrified to think that he had in any way withstood the desires of one who was more than father and mother to him: the whole Kala'at was the Consul's, a free gift, a thing not to be mentioned between them. The Consul refused the gift, but agreed to purchase, and with Ali's blessing on his head went to intercede with the authorities; as if by magic the prison doors were opened, and without trial or question Ali was a free man again. In return for an embroidered cloak, a pair of blue leather boots, and a revolver (the last for Hassan, Ali's eldest son) the British Government acquired an undefined quarter share in the site of the Hittite capital, and a formal deed of sale and ownership was enregistered in the Land Office at Birijik.

When in 1911 the new expedition took the field Ali was long dead, and Hassan Agha his son, now an old man, reigned in his room. He fully recognized the British rights, but as the quarter share was undefined and no one could say over which part of the Kala'at work would extend, a fresh agreement was drawn up. A flat low-lying area within the town walls, which was arable and therefore of some value, was not to be disturbed except by special arrangement: common grazing might continue as heretofore, but over the rest of the ruin-encumbered ground the excavators had a perfectly free hand for as long as they cared to work; and in consideration of certain moneys received Hassan relinquished all claim to any objects in the working area. He was quite anxious to sell the whole site outright for a mere song—for he made nothing out of it—but as the work was still in the experimental stage this offer could not be accepted.

In 1912 the construction of the Bagdad Railway had begun: German engineers were at Jerablus, and rumour ran that every landowner along the line would make his fortune. Hassan now offered us the site at a figure running into thousands, and when we laughed at him he sulked:—poor old man! his last wife had drowned herself in the river, and he wanted to marry again, but the younger members of his house declared unfeelingly that he was far too old and refused to advance the necessary cash. Accordingly we resumed work on the terms of the agreement made the year before: Hassan feebly urged that the "consideration" paid to him then should be renewed with every season, but confronted with the text of his bargain was reduced to silence.

Now the hardest and most costly part of our work was that of removing to a distance, where they would not hamper future digging, the mass of broken stones which covered the surface and lay thick in the upper strata of the soil. Close by were the German engineers, busily building houses and hospitals, and hard put to it to find rubble for their foundations. It was a great chance, and I at once agreed with the Germans that they should at their expense carry off from our work all the stones they wanted; and soon we had the satisfaction of seeing a whole procession of carts and donkeys shifting our spoil-heaps and making easy our future excavations.

Then Hassan Agha came to me with a grievance. These stones were being given away gratis, whereas he might have sold them to the Germans for a good price: could not I get the Germans to pay for them? I went to the chief engineer, who at once refused: the stones, weathered by exposure, were not really good for building, though better than none: the cost of carriage represented their full value to him, and if he had to pay he would prefer to leave them alone and get his stones from the newly-opened quarries on the hill-side beyond the railway. When I told Hassan this he was much upset, the more so because all the village laughed at him: he talked loudly of his grievance, and being one day in Birijik voiced it there also; some one carried the tale to the Kaimmakam, who saw his chance, and sending for Hassan Agha he hatched with him the plot that was to form Act the Second in our comedy.

One day a soldier rode up to our tents with a written message for Lawrence. It was a summons for him to stand his trial before the Sheri' Court of Birijik on the charge of having stolen from the plaintiff, Hassan Agha, certain property, stones to wit, which he had sold for the sum of thirty Turkish pounds to the chief engineer of the Jerablus section of the Bagdad Railway.

Now, under the Capitulations, no British subject can be tried by any Turkish Court unless the British Consul be represented on the bench: moreover, the

Sheri' Court in particular is a religious tribunal for administering laws founded on the Koran, and applying to Moslems alone, so that in no circumstances can a foreigner be cited before it. The present summons was therefore doubly illegal, and could safely have been disregarded: but Lawrence and I discussed the point, and—for we did not then suspect the Kaimmakam's finger in the pie—decided that it might be better for him to appear: the charge was so silly that it could be disposed of at once, and also, living as we did in the country and on close terms with the people, we were not altogether anxious to shelter ourselves behind such privileges as attached to us merely as foreigners: if Hassan thought he had a legal grievance we would answer him, not by evading the law, but by availing ourselves of it.

On the day appointed, therefore, Lawrence rode over to Birijik and took his place in the dock. After protesting that he only attended by courtesy a tribunal that had no legal jurisdiction, he denied the charge, and produced in support of his denial a statement from myself, claiming all responsibility for what was done on the work, and therefore exculpating him, an affidavit from the German chief engineer to the effect that he had not and would not pay a penny for the stones removed by him, the original firman authorizing our excavations, and the agreement signed by Hassan Agha relinquishing all rights to anything within their area. All these papers were promptly impounded by the court. Then the

THE KAIMMAKAM OF BIRIJIK

counsel for the prosecution got up and stated that the stones had indubitably been sold, in proof whereof he was prepared to bring into court sixteen witnesses, all Arab workmen from Jerablus, who would swear to the details of a conversation alleged to have taken place (*in French !*) between Lawrence and the German: he therefore asked that the case be remanded for a week. Before Lawrence could object, the remand had been granted and the court adjourned.

Lawrence came back in a state of great disgust, and I was no better pleased, especially when village gossip brought us the news that Hassan Agha was only a half-hearted tool in the hands of the Kaimmakam; and then we realized that the court— in other words, the Governor—was in possession of all the documents on which we depended for authority to work at all. In view of this I decided that I should attend the next hearing with Lawrence and insist on the farce being brought to a close. In the meantime digging continued as usual, and the stones about which so much fuss was being made were still being carried off for the new buildings by the railway. This was perhaps rather in the nature of contempt of court, and we were hardly surprised when half-way through the week an attempt was made to stop it.

The Kaimmakam sent orders to his onbashi at Jerablus that the Germans were not to remove stones from our work, and accordingly the soldiers took up their position at the Kala'at gate and forcibly held up all the carts and donkeys. The chief engineer, much worried, came down to me to talk over ways and means. I suggested that he should make over all his transport gang to me and give me their wages in a lump sum, whereupon I would myself have the stones carted off and dumped down handy for his buildings. He agreed thankfully, and we called the donkey-men together and told them that they were now in my employ, and having made them load up I walked at the head of the string out from the Kala'at. The onbashi—a good fellow—dashed forward to stop me. I asked him what he meant by it, and he replied that his orders were to stop the Germans taking stones.

"Do so, then," I answered, "but don't interrupt *me*: this is my gang, and your orders say nothing about my carrying my stones where I please."

The drivers gleefully corroborated the statement that they had changed masters: the onbashi was puzzled, but said that it seemed to amount to the same thing, and he must carry out the spirit of his orders.

I said, "Would you go beyond the letter of them if I were to use force on my side?"

He smiled. "Oh no!" he said; "please use force, Effendim; that will put me all right with the Kaimmakam."

So I solemnly drew a revolver and pointed it at him, and he as solemnly marched in front of me to where the hospital foundations were being laid, and we dumped our stones on the heap which the Germans had already piled there.

"Very good," he said. "I shall of course have to report to Birijik that you have forcibly prevented my doing what I suppose is my duty: but you know that I'm very glad not to be a nuisance."

We shook hands, smoked cigarettes together while the next load of stones came up, and parted the best of friends, I to go back to the diggings and he to write his report. So that was the end of that move in the game, for the Kaimmakam sent no further orders to Jerablus.

The day fixed for the re-hearing of our trial saw us riding again to Birijik, with Haj Wahid, in his rôle of interpreter once more, tricked out in his best clothes, with two revolvers stuck in the voluminous folds of his silk sash and a carbine over his shoulder to add to his importance. Half-way on our journey we met no less a person than Hassan Agha himself riding towards Jerablus. Asked why he was thus going in the wrong direction the plaintiff told us that the case was not going to be heard that day: moreover he had washed his hands of the whole affair, so that we need not bother to go to Birijik at all. Hassan was obviously ill at ease, and as we had received no notice of the trial having been postponed we determined to continue on our way and find out the truth for ourselves; so on we went, and, arriving at the town, proceeded at once to pay a call upon the Kaimmakam.

That slippery gentleman greeted us with the utmost goodwill, ordered in coffee and cigarettes, inquired with interest after the progress of our digging, and at last asked why we had left them to come to town and whether he could be of any service to us. I told him that he could: that we had come in answer to a summons from his court and that we wished the matter to be settled now and for good and all. The Governor was deeply distressed. He had heard of the case and had recognized at once that it was purely malicious and absurd: if only we had written to him he would have settled it at once and saved us the trouble of our journey; but since we had come and had been so happily inspired as to call upon him he would do anything we wanted. I suggested that he might send for the Cadi and inform him that to-day's hearing must decide the matter, as it was a perfectly straightforward one and we could not keep on neglecting our work to attend the court; he agreed at once, sent for the Cadi and talked to him privately for a while, then assured us that everything was arranged and that in case of any difficulty in court we had only to send for him and he would come at once. We left him with thanks and made room for a seedy-looking individual whom Lawrence recognized as counsel for the prosecution—then, after a lunch in the town, we went to stand our trial.

The court-house was in the Serai, opening off the same balcony as gave access to the Kaimmakam's office, a fair-sized room already crowded with an audience anxious to hear the trial of the two Englishmen. The Cadi took his seat at a desk on a raised dais accompanied by two assessors, while a clerk at a

THE KAIMMAKAM OF BIRIJIK 169

table below him made voluminous notes. We took our places facing him and close to the door.

As soon as the case was opened (by proclamation of the usher) I got up and, through Haj Wahid, informed the judge that if any charge was brought in connection with the excavations it could only be directed against myself, not Lawrence. I pointed out that his court had no jurisdiction over us, but said that we had hitherto waived the point out of courtesy, and were prepared to overlook it now should the case be reasonably conducted, but that if any further delay were interposed we should at once appeal to the only court which could legally try us, namely, that of Aleppo. The Cadi agreed that the charge implicated me as well as Lawrence, and noted the warning of appeal. Then I pointed out that our evidence was already in the hands of the court and was quite sufficient to decide the issue: on the other hand, the prosecution, who had asked for a week's remand to produce witnesses, had not even warned these to appear—in fact the witnesses had no intention of coming, and if they came could not give the evidence promised, as they knew no French: that the prosecutor was not in court and had washed his hands of the case, and that not a shred of evidence had been or could be brought against us. After this the counsel for the prosecution jumped up and asked —without giving reasons—for a week's remand! Of course I objected: the counsel repeated his request; and after a consultation between Cadi and assessors the court was cleared of the public, only Lawrence and I remaining behind. Then there was a long confabulation on the Bench and a lengthy document was drawn up by the clerk, after which the doors were opened and the public flocked in again. The Cadi read out the document, and, sending it across to me, asked me to sign it; naturally I inquired what it was, and after a little difficulty had it explained—it was to the effect that I agreed to a remand being granted.

This was thoroughly annoying. I got up again and told the Cadi that I refused to sign, or to agree to anything of the sort: on the contrary, seeing how things were being run, I now refused to recognize the legality of the trial and appealed to Aleppo. "So far as I am concerned," I said, "the case is over: I shall not attend the court again, and I must ask you to return to me at once all the papers that have been handed in to you."

The Cadi replied that papers impounded by the court remained in its possession till the conclusion of the case.

"But the case *is* concluded," I urged, "and I must have my papers."

The Cadi again refused. Then I remembered the Kaimmakam's promise and determined to put it to the test. "The Kaimmakam," I said, "has promised me to come himself here should any difficulty arise : will you kindly send for him?"

The Cadi smiled and sent the usher into the next room; in a few seconds the usher returned to say that the Kaimmakam was sorry but could not come. The Cadi smiled broadly and the court began to laugh out loud.

The trick that was being played upon us, and the Governor's part in it, was now quite clear, and as long as they held our precious documents—he could destroy them if he liked—I was at his mercy. So again I said, " Will you give me back my papers ? " and again the Cadi said no, adding in his official tone as he picked up the books on his desk, " The case is remanded till this day next week."

" Well," I said, " I'm not going to leave this room until I get them."

The Cadi smiled again. " In that case," said he, " you will not leave till next week at least."

Amid the laughter that rewarded this jest I turned to Haj Wahid and told him to clear out, as there was going to be trouble and he, as an Ottoman subject, might get the worst of it : but the Haj was spoiling for a fight and disdained the idea of leaving his masters in the lurch ; " Eib, Effendim, Eib "— the disgrace of it ! he kept repeating, and swore by his father's bones that nothing would move him. So I rose again, and levelling a revolver at the Cadi, who by this time was also on his feet, I said, " *You* will not leave the room alive at all unless I get those papers." The Cadi dropped back into his seat like a rabbit, and Haj Wahid, with a revolver in each hand, was vaguely threatening any one who caught his eye.

" Lawrence," I said, " bolt into the next room and hold up the Kaimmakam: I bet the old brute's got the papers himself." Lawrence darted through the door: the usher seized the chance of disappearing after him, and that gave the signal for a general *sauve qui peut*: the public and the assessors and the Clerk of the Court jammed in the doorway for an instant, then melted away, and only Haj Wahid and myself were left with the Cadi, crouched as low as he could get in his official throne. I lowered my weapon and told Haj Wahid to keep the door: the judge looked intensely relieved, and, finding some French for the occasion, begged me to come and sit on the recently-vacated chair beside him and to take a cigarette. I complied, and we had sat for a minute or two in rather uncomfortable silence, the judge still eyeing the revolver I was nursing, when Lawrence reappeared.

"I've got the papers," he announced, "the blighter had them all in his own desk!"

"Did he make any difficulty?" I asked.

"Oh no. When I got in he handed them over like a lamb. But he says he'd like to have a copy of the Hassan Agha contract made, and" (at this point Lawrence broke down) "would you oblige him with the penny stamp?"

It was almost the best joke of the lot, and I paid cheerfully; then, the copy having been made, I pocketed the original papers, shook hands with the Cadi, and left the court.

But when we came out on the balcony we had to stop and laugh again. The terror-stricken audience from the court-house had spread far and wide the

THE KAIMMAKAM OF BIRIJIK 173

news of how we were holding up the executive of the province, and of course the first to hear it had been the soldiers in the Serai. They felt that it was up to them to do something, but there had been no shots, no calls for help from their superiors, and they had collected in the courtyard, excited, but uncertain where their duty lay. When we appeared at the top of the staircase, obviously victorious—Haj Wahid's swagger as he came behind us twisting a ferocious moustache with one hand while the other played with the revolvers in his belt was of itself enough to show who had won the day — then the Oriental asserted itself: automatically the soldiers fell into line and stood stiffly at the salute as we passed between the files! We walked through the bazaar, the shopkeepers coming forward to salaam, and murmurs of "Wallah!" and "Mashallah!" rising on either side, and so crossed the ferry and rode back to Jerablus in triumph.

I may add that the whole thing was reported to Aleppo, and the local Minister for Foreign Affairs there went round in a great state of mind to see our Consul, who had already received a report from myself.

"Those English of yours at Jerablus," began the excited Turk, "they are doing impossible things—perfectly impossible: why, they have tried to shoot the Governor and the Cadi of the Province!"

"Did they really shoot them?" inquired the Consul.

"Well, no, they *threatened* to, but they did not actually *kill* them."

"What a pity," the Consul remarked gently. And the Minister did not pursue the subject.

About two months later Hogarth came out from Oxford to visit us, and having occasion to go to Birijik he paid a call upon the Kaimmakam and took the opportunity of referring to our trial, expressing the hope that as nothing more had been heard about it the whole matter had blown over. The Kaimmakam assured him that the regrettable incident was quite a thing of the past: he had used his authority to quash a case which ought never to have been brought—which none but an ignorant peasant would ever have brought against us, and he begged Hogarth—and ourselves, for whom he professed the warmest feelings—to forget the whole thing. That evening—it was a Saturday—Hogarth returned to camp and congratulated us on the end of a vexatious affair.

On the Sunday afternoon following, a regular procession was seen advancing across the Kala'at towards our house: the court usher of Birijik came first, then about ten soldiers, then Hassan Agha and his son, and a little crowd of the idle and curious. I was rather busy, but went out at last and was asked to listen to a long Turkish rigmarole which the usher began to read from two closely-written pages of foolscap. I cut him short and demanded what it was all about, and learned—I was sincerely sorry that Hogarth happened to be out—that it was the verdict on our trial. The case had continued in our contumacious absence, and we had been found guilty: I was to pay forthwith to the prosecutor the sum of thirty pounds and costs, to close down all excavations, and not to resume work until a fresh firman had been obtained from Constantinople and a new contract drawn up with Hassan Agha; the usher with his men had come to collect the money and pay it to Hassan on the spot, and to put a stop to my digging.

"Does the paper really say all that?" I asked, and, being assured that it really did, inquired whether I might have it. The portentous document was at once handed over, and I promptly tore it into small pieces, much to the horror of the usher, who saw the Sultan's signature printed at the top go neatly in halves. "There," I said, "that's the end of that. I'm not going to pay a penny to Hassan or any one, I'm not going to make a new contract, and as for stopping work, I'll re-start to-morrow with more men than ever. Now, is there any one here who wants a job or would like to recommend a friend?"

One of the soldiers of the usher's escort spoke up. "Effendim," he said, "would you take on my brother?"

"Certainly," I answered, "send him along early to-morrow." And the procession went disconsolately back across the Kala'at and embarked for Birijik. That was the end of the matter, but it gave us a certain amount of satisfaction, for Lawrence and I are probably the only foreigners alive who have been tried and condemned by the Sheri' Courts of Turkey.

I am afraid that a somewhat distorted version of

the affair must have got abroad, for when shortly afterwards I went to Constantinople my reception by our then Ambassador was hardly cordial: he seemed to think that our action had been altogether too drastic, and told me that Turkey was a civilized country. However, I saw to it that the Kaimmakam received such an official wigging as made him regret the part that he had played, nor did he ever trouble us again.

But a word must be added about poor old Hassan. Our commissaire, Fuad Bey, annoyed at the trouble he had caused, raised the question of the real ownership of the Kala'at, and a Commission was appointed to look into this. The Commissioners took up a plea which had formerly been urged by the Turkish War Office to oppose our application for a digging permit,—the plea that Carchemish had been a military stronghold, that it was still known as the Kala'at or Fort of Jerablus, and that by law no Turkish fortress could become the property of an individual nor could the right of examining it be granted to foreigners. In spite of the argument which we had successfully employed that no fort had stood there since Roman times, the new Commission decided that Carchemish was the inalienable property of the State and that its registration as private property had been fraudulent: the British Museum waived its quarter right, and Hassan was arbitrarily ousted from the rest—all, that is, save the low-lying tilth which could not be brought within the Turkish definition of a Kala'at. Of course it was a hardship, not to say an injustice, of which we were ultimately the cause, so when all was settled above our heads we made Hassan a present of the sum for which he had originally offered to sell us the whole site; it was a very popular act, considered by everybody to be characteristically English, and it bound Hassan Agha to us as a most penitent friend.

A CHIEF OF THE KURDS

CROSS the Euphrates from Jerablus and you find yourself in a country of rolling grassy steppes, treeless and waterless, which reaches eastwards to the Tigris and northwards to the hills of Diarbekir and Nisibin. Here and there are rocky outcrops of limestone or basalt; steep-banked *wadies*, dry nearly all the year round, intersect the country, but there are few outstanding features to break its sameness. The wide prairies, over which the spring rains spread a shimmering carpet of grass and short-stemmed flowers, lie all summer long parched to a weary brown, unrelieved and never-ending, and in winter turn to brown mud reaches or are shrouded under short-lived snow. But there is a fine spaciousness about these stony down-lands: the wind blows free across them, whether from the north-western mountains or from the far Persian hills, finding nothing to stay its course, and though the sun may be a burden at mid-day, yet the nights are fresh and cool, there is a vigour in the air and a glory of sunrise and of sunset, a beauty of far-flung moonlight across valley and rise which not even the arid deserts of Egypt can outdo.

Over this wide tract wander the Milli-Kurds. Less differentiated than most Kurdish tribes from the old Persian stock, they are new-comers here, whose migration indeed is scarcely ended yet, for they are still by slow degrees pushing before them farther and farther west the Arabs who had held this North Mesopotamian fringe, and villages which but ten years ago were purely Arab are to-day in Kurdish hands. Their language is a dialect of Persian, though most of the men are bi-lingual and speak either Arabic or Turkish, according as their movements bring them in touch with the one or the other people on their borders. A nomad race, their riches lie in herds of sheep and goats and in the horses of which they are vastly proud; in the spring-time they till after a fashion the valley-bottoms, growing grain enough to keep their households and their live-stock through the coming year, but they have no hankering after the settled farming life. A few chiefs boast builded houses set in some richer valley and surrounded by the huts of their immediate followers, huts which, thanks to the scarcity of roofing-timber, are built in fashion like tall bee-hives or like the giant ant-heaps of Africa, of mud-brick throughout from ground-level to the top of the cone; but even the chiefs, so soon as summer sets in, are glad to leave the bondage of stone walls and to wander forth over the open country, pitching their tents where fancy wills and striking camp again when sojourn in one place irks their roving spirit. Their tents are of black goat's-hair cloth, closely woven to keep out the rare rain, hung on a row of upright poles, with shorter props along the sides to give head-room: by the number of a man's tent-poles you can judge his wealth and rank—from the one- or two-poled shelter of the common clansman to the moving palace of a tribal chief with its twenty or thirty poles and living-room for half a hundred people. Inside, the tent is divided by curtains into the closed women's quarters, the main room where the men-folk sleep and eat and meet their friends; and often too the half-open space at one end which serves as stable and byre; those of the rich are hung along the sides with coloured "killims" woven by the women, their fine patterns too often disfigured to our eyes by tags of every sort of fancy cloth knotted tassel-wise into the web.

The women are seldom veiled, and unless you are actually a guest in the tent—in which case they stay discreetly hidden—are little shy of strangers. Bigly made for the most part, with a high colour and features bold but not unpleasing, crowned by masses of black hair worn in heavy braids, none too cleanly perhaps, and dressed clumsily but in brilliant colours, they are a cheerful and a hospitable crew, though at times embarrassingly curious as to how an Englishman's clothes take off and on. The men dress like the Arabs, with whom indeed they are on friendly terms, united by a common hatred of the Turk; good riders, often hard drinkers and professing the faith of Mohammed but at heart, recking little of any religion, devoted to all games

A CHIEF OF THE KURDS

of skill and to the chase, gamblers who will cheerfully stake their last coin and even the liberty of their persons on a throw of the dice, cruel and treacherous—for they will break even the bond of hospitality which Bedouin honour holds sacred—music-loving, great dancers, money-grabbers and yet spending their all on personal finery, boastful and suspicious, thieves by open profession to whom robbery is as honourable as ever it was held to be on the Scottish Marches, and as fond of a practical joke as is an undergraduate—one may condemn them as a bad lot, but as sportsmen and as good company one must needs like them well.

The polity of the Milli-Kurds is patriarchal. They are divided into twelve main tribes or *ashiret*, subdivided into clans or households more or less straitly organized as families congregate yearly in some richer valley for the spring sowing or wander in isolated freedom over the less fertile uplands. The headship of the *ashira* is hereditary, but does not descend always by right of primogeniture: from the ruling house the tribes elect that member whose abilities point him out as most likely to make a good sheikh, and do not hesitate to pass over the eldest son. The chief so chosen is far from being the untrammelled master of his people: not only are all domestic matters, such as those pertaining to women-kind, ruled altogether out of his province—for in these, unless they involve wider issues, the head of the household has the final say, and at most the chief may be invited to arbitrate between families at feud—but he has no force to compel the sheikh of a clan who may dispute his orders; democracy is the key-note of his rule, and while he may be absolute enough so long as he stands for the received traditions of the race, yet when he would venture on a line of his own choosing he must commend this to the minds of his people before he can rely on their obedience. Indeed, that their loyalty is none too hard and fast a bond, but rather a matter of convenience sanctioned by use, is shown by the fact that an able sheikh of a tribe, whose rule makes for prosperity, will attract to himself men of other tribes, and these seem to transfer their allegiance without incurring objection or reproach. The authority which binds together nomad folk must always be a loose one, affecting the individual but lightly, for personal freedom is at once the condition and the object of their manner of life; only by some pressure from without, such as drought or persecution, or else by the uprising of a 'great natural leader who knows how to turn their combined strength to profitable ends, can real unity and a common cause be for a time imposed upon them.

At the end of last century all the Milli-Kurd tribes were united under one leader, Ibrahim Pasha, who in his lifetime was the *beau idéal* of his race, and since his death has become almost a legendary hero. His tent of forty poles was hung with rich embroideries outside and in. When he would shift his camp the women rose betimes and in hurried silence stripped down the heavy hangings and rolled

A CHIEF OF THE KURDS

them up, took down the poles, packed all upon the hundred camels which formed his constant baggage-train, and stole away before the light. So when the sun woke the men-folk, lo! all the paraphernalia of the great camp had melted away as if by magic, their horses, stalled the night before, now stood tethered in the open, and they needed but to mount and ride away as if all the world were out-of-doors and tents undreamt of. A hundred and twenty cavaliers formed the Pasha's bodyguard, and these never left him. At any moment the forward march could be changed into a race, or stopped for a *jereed* — the sham-fight which the Kurd loves. His falconers rode in his train ready to slip the jesses and let fly the hawks at any game that showed. Did he wish coffee, as the Kurd does at all hours, he had but to clap his hands and the *gahwaji* would gallop up, the brazier with its boiling pot and the tray of little cups slung like kettledrums on either side of his saddle, and would pour and hand to his lord without need even to slacken pace.

The Pasha was very wealthy, and prodigal as became his station. It is told of him that one day in the silk khan of Aleppo he wished to buy himself an embroidered cloak. The shopkeeper produced one, and when asked the price replied that it was five pounds; Ibrahim called up a porter who was loitering on the far side of the courtyard, and tossed over to him the unworthy garment. A second cloak was shown of double the value: Ibrahim turned to one of his followers and asked whether he would accept it. A third, better and more costly, was given to a chief of his suite; and it was only when an "aba" of gold and silver tissue, valued at some thirty pounds, was brought out for his inspection, and he was assured that there was none finer or of greater price in Aleppo, that the Pasha felt himself fitted. To the Kurd or Arab, who will bargain for two days over a piastre, there is something truly royal in a magnificence that will neither dispute a price nor even refuse goods once offered lest the refusal be read as meanness.

The Milli-Kurds have never acknowledged a more than formal allegiance to Turkey, and Turkey has left them fairly well to their own devices: in particular, they have successfully stood out against all liability to army service. Abdul Hamid, however, towards the end of his reign suggested that they should enrol themselves as tribal horsemen under their own chiefs in the irregular force of "Hamidieh," which the astute Sultan was raising throughout his dominions, a force owning loyalty only to the person of the Sultan himself, and designed to uphold him against any revolt on the part of his other subjects. Ibrahim Pasha was quite willing to accept the offer. It did not interfere with but rather strengthened the tribal organization, it introduced no foreign element, and it enabled him to arm and equip his followers without rousing the suspicion of the Government. Indeed, at this time Ibrahim was but little less than an independent monarch. He was rich; he had, if not a standing

A CHIEF OF THE KURDS

army, at least the power of calling up an armed *levée en masse* such as no Turkish Government would care to provoke; his territory was practically inviolate, for no tax-gatherers and no troops dared show their faces on the wide steppes; and his people owed no fealty to the Turkish overlord save through his own person. On the northern confines of the desert, at Wiranshehr, he built a capital for himself, bringing in thither Arab and Armenian settlers, and he even showed his broad-mindedness by setting up an Armenian bishop in the new town; he had no idea of himself abandoning the nomadic life, but he saw the advantages of having a fixed seat of government and a commercial centre for the produce of his own country.

The revolution that overthrew Abdul Hamid came about too suddenly for the Hamidieh to fulfil their rôle; but Ibrahim Pasha was quite willing to do his part, taken by surprise though he was, and he rallied his tribesmen in arms to strike a blow for the old order. Unfortunately for him the new Government was ready: troops were sent out from Aleppo, and at Tel Bashar near the Euphrates, twenty miles from Jerablus, met and scattered the Hamidieh levies before the mobilization was complete. Then the Young Turks sent envoys to the Pasha, requesting him to come in for an interview at which they might explain to him the ideals of the Committee, the justice of its cause, and the liberality of its intentions. Ibrahim came in to the enemy's camp, but, being warned that his murder was arranged, slipped away and prepared to organize a fresh resistance. Again the envoys were sent to find him and reproached him with his want of faith in the Young Turk party; treachery and murder were the very features of the old regime, against which the Revolution was a protest, and a talk with the local leaders of the Committee would convince him that in the new-born age of liberty, the *Huriet*, he had nothing to fear from its champions. The Pasha let himself be convinced; he came in to a conference with the Young Turks, who received him cordially, and with a cup of poisoned coffee settled his last scruples.

Ibrahim Pasha being dead, the Milli-Kurds had no further powers of resistance. A punitive force from Aleppo harried their country and laid waste the town of Wiranshehr, and Ibrahim's sons, who were still but boys, were seized and carried off as hostages; lacking a common leader, the chief tribes broke up their confederacy, and in the feuds which soon set them at loggerheads with one another gave to the Government the best of guarantees against future trouble.

I had only been a short time at Jerablus when I received a visit from Busrawi Agha, certainly to-day the most prominent of the sheikhs who, not being Milli, yet once adhered to their alliance. A man of about forty-five, of medium height and heavy build, with a broad intellectual face and a pleasant expression, he is a good specimen of his people, and if he shares most of their faults, he has also more good qualities than most. He was the second son of his father, but succeeded to the chieftainship on the score of diplomatic gifts, his brains outweighing his elder brother's better record as a fighting man. The choice was justified by the event, for Busrawi has raised the prestige of his *ashira* far above what it was in his father's time, so that now not only Kurds of other tribes but even many Arabs are proud to boast of him as their overlord. He claims to have control over 4000 tents, a tent meaning anything from one man to ten, and the vast majority of his followers are mounted and, after a fashion, armed: but it would be difficult to say how many of these he could count upon to answer his summons in case of war. As I have said before, the patriarchal system, based on the unit of the family, has a greater influence on the Kurds than has the more complex organization of the tribe, and men own a more direct obedience to the head of their own clan than to the sheikh of their *ashira*. The allegiance of the heads of the clans, especially since the break-up of Ibrahim Pasha's confederacy, is a doubtful matter, largely one of convenience, and any one of them is free to defy his superior, provided that the strength of his following or the remoteness of his grazing-grounds give warrant for defiance. In fact, a Kurdish chief must walk delicately if he would rule and yet not alienate his people, and it is much to the credit of Busrawi's tact that he has not only held his power but increased it.

When in the Balkan War the Bulgarians reached the Chataldja lines, and the whole empire stood on tip-toe expecting the capital to fall, the Milli-Kurds saw a chance to revenge Ibrahim's death. Under the leadership of some of the murdered Pasha's family the scheme was formed of attacking Aleppo as soon as the news of Stamboul's capture should have announced the collapse of Turkish power. The plan affected me closely, for the line of march proposed by the Kurds was through Jerablus, and as they promised openly to cut the throats of all the Germans on the Bagdad line between Aleppo and the river, I felt that my own position might be none too secure. So I asked Busrawi to come in and see me, and laid the difficulty before him; but he scouted the idea of any danger to myself, and said that if I liked he would put a guard of two thousand men on the place, so that I might continue my work without hindrance. I took this opportunity of inquiring how large a force he proposed taking with him for the attack upon the vilayet, and, in view of the reputed number of his followers, was interested to hear that he would have no more than five thousand; he assured me that this was because the contingents from all the tribes were to be proportionate, but I cannot help thinking that in fact he would have found it hard to raise a greater force sufficiently well armed to encounter the regular troops of Turkey.

The Kurds were looking forward with no little pleasure to the sack of so rich a city as Aleppo, and being one day in the town, I was much amused to meet both Busrawi's eldest son and one of the Shahin Bey brothers, joint rulers of the neighbouring *ashira*: they both gave at the outset very lame excuses for their visits to Aleppo, and it was only when I taxed them with it directly that they admitted their real object, which was no other than the drawing up of lists of such houses as would yield the best plunder. Constantinople did not fall, so the raid never took place; but this anxiety to get in first for the loot led to a queer incident, which, though it has nothing to do with Busrawi, I will quote here for the light it throws on Kurdish character.

Derai was then the leader of a small tribe, the Karagetch. An ignorant and a brutal man, low in the councils of the chiefs, he felt that he might be worsted when it came to the division of the spoil, and determined therefore to be first on the spot. With his contingent of 945 men he marched to Birijik and quartered himself upon the town, taking what he would from the bazaar without ceremony of purchase, and generally terrorizing the inhabitants. One night a false alarm reached Birijik that Stamboul had fallen: the Kaimmakam proclaimed the news from the Serai, the Mullahs indulged in lamentation from the minarets, and Derai crossed the Euphrates. He had not gone far on his way—was in fact billeted on the little town of Nizib—when he learned that the rumour was false. While he was stopping there, undecided how to act, officers sent out from Aleppo arrived and demanded to know what he was doing with an armed force on the western side of the river. Derai, alone and unsupported, answered with innocent surprise that he was doing what any patriotic subject would do—hurrying to put himself and his followers at the disposal of the Government against the foreign invader; he was as surprised as he was chagrined when he was taken at his word and told, with thanks, that he would be sent at once to the front. A few days later he was ordered to proceed to Aintab. As he was leaving Nizib he was overtaken by an officer in uniform who, saluting, said that he had been appointed medical officer to the Kurdish contingent, and had come in to report. Derai, taking the man's papers, inquired who and what he was, and learning that he was an Armenian doctor, turned about and ordered his men to shoot him there and then. The thing was done, and Derai sent back a messenger into the town with orders that the body be not moved from the roadway where it lay, but be left to testify to the Sheikh's attitude towards all unbelievers.

Derai's battalion was first sent to Constantinople, but as they began by laughing at the Turkish major who was sent to drill them, and then when they found that he was serious stoned him out of their camp, they were dispatched to Gallipoli, where the Bulgarians were threatening the Bulair lines. Their only deed of arms was when one day they were ordered to advance against the enemy forces entrenched upon a hill to the north: the wild horsemen galloped forward in true Kurdish fashion, blazing away with their rifles in the air and shouting as they rode, but

A CHIEF OF THE KURDS

coming under the Bulgars' shrapnel-fire retired more hastily than they went, declaring that this was no civilized warfare. Found to be useless here, they were shifted again into the Ismid peninsula, where they profitably employed themselves in plundering the refugees from the conquered European provinces, and finally, on the conclusion of peace, returned to Mesopotamia laden with booty taken from the Turks.

The Kurd is in fact a desert warrior, absolutely unsuited, by temperament as well as by tradition, to modern methods of warfare. He is not lacking in courage in his own way, but his wars, like those of the Bedouin, are pleasure parties, marked by more noise than bloodshed. For nearly thirty years there was a standing feud between the tribe of Busrawi and that of Shahin Bey, a feud which, kept in check by Ibrahim Pasha, broke out into regular tribal warfare after his death. The usual course of mutual raiding, cattle-lifting, and murder was aggravated by the fact that the winter houses of the rival chiefs lay but some ten miles apart at the far ends of the same fertile valley. On one occasion, hearing that Busrawi was away and only a scanty guard left in his village, Shahin Bey determined to strike a blow which would cripple his enemy; he would attack the village in overwhelming force, destroy the chief's house, and make his wife and sons prisoners. Preparations were made in all secrecy, and it was only on the day set for the attack that Busrawi's elder brother, left in charge at home, heard from a panic-stricken messenger that Shahin with more than a thousand mounted men was at that moment advancing against him. The hurried alarm brought together a hundred and twenty men, all that could be mustered in so short a space, and counsel was divided; but there was no time to get their households clear away, and it was, too great a disgrace to abandon the Sheikh's house to the enemy. In the open space amongst the houses—the village dancing-floor—the little band sat on the ground and wept for the tribe's shame to come. Then (I had the story from one of the actors in it) the Sheikh's brother rose and pointed to the growing dust-cloud in the distance that betrayed Shahin's advance. "We can only die," he told them; "let us at least die well. Take your horses, and mount in close order. Throw away your guns and tie your head-cloths over your faces that you may not see Death coming, and charge, knee to knee, with the sword."[1] They mounted, and they waited till the enemy came close, his horsemen breaking rank to wheel this way or that, waving their rifles, shooting in the air, and yelling for their easy victory. They waited in silence, and they charged without a sound. "We smote them all together like a stone, and like a stone we broke them," said the teller of the tale. It was a new thing in Kurdish fighting, these blinded men who came on so quietly, and they cut their way through the enemy who had not looked

[1] Compare the exhortation of Zeid to the Arabs at the battle of Yemāna, A.D. 632, as he led the charge against the Beni Hanīfa, "Close your eyes and clench your teeth. Forward like men!"

for resistance—turned and cut through again, and then—then tore off their bandages to see half a dozen of Shahin's men dead on the ground and the rest, with many wounded among them, scattered in panic along the track for home. Such fighting savours rather of the tourney than of the butchery of a modern battle-field, but such is Kurdish warfare, the *jereed* played in earnest, the best of games for men.

The feud between the two tribes, which after Shahin Bey's death was carried on by his two sons, ended in a, for me, dramatic scene. I had just finished breakfast one morning when I was told that the two Shahins were outside and wished to see me. As it chanced that a lady missionary on her way up-country had stopped the night with us, and it would have been a breach of etiquette to bring the chiefs into the room where she was, I had to ask them to sit outside with Haj Wahid for company until the lady was safely on her way. When she had gone, and we were all inside busy with coffee and cigarettes, Midai, my Kurd house-guard, beckoned me to the door and whispered that Busrawi was to be expected at any moment. I was more than a little nervous, as I knew all about the feud and had no wish to see it brought to a head in my sitting-room; so I went out again and suggested to Midai that he might meet Busrawi and get him to put off his visit till the afternoon. But Midai, with a portentous secrecy which made his whispers almost unintelligible, assured me that it was all right and that the chief's coming was timed on purpose; but I was still feeling very uneasy when word was brought that Busrawi was on his way across the Kala'at.

I went out and met him in the courtyard. This, by the way, is a nicely calculated compliment: the ordinary native walks into your room and you do not leave your chair; to a greater one you rise, or go to meet him at the door if you would do him honour; a head chief you may go out to meet as an equal in the courtyard; but as an Englishman you must not, in welcome or at leave-taking, go beyond the entrance of the court, for that would stamp you as the inferior of your guest. Busrawi was dressed in his best, not gaudily, but as befitted a chief—I put down his head-cloth as costing eight pounds, and his cloak was well worth double that sum: with him was a big stoutish Kurd, also well-dressed in Bagdad fashion, a stranger to me, and, as I learnt later, a cousin of Ibrahim Pasha; two of Busrawi's personal following completed the group.

I welcomed the sheikhs, and, still wondering what line I was to take regarding their enemies seated inside, led them to the sitting-room. The two Shahins rose to their feet: Busrawi's party stood silent by the door. I took the bull by the horns. "Busrawi Agha," I said, "I want you to meet my friends the sons of Shahin Bey. Busrawi Agha—Shahin Bey," and I pointed to the elder of the two brothers and anxiously wondered what would happen next. The two looked at each other, then slowly stepped forward and held out their hands: Busrawi drew the younger man towards him and kissed him

BUSRAWI (IN THE CENTRE) WITH TWO MINOR CHIEFS.

solemnly on both cheeks, then he saluted the younger Shahin in like manner. Every one—not only I— gave a sigh of relief, and we sat down all together, while Midai, beaming with smiles, handed coffee to the reconciled chiefs. Then Ibrahim's cousin made a speech: he said that this meeting, which was ardently desired by the Milli - Kurd leaders, and was most necessary with a view to uniting Arabs and Kurds alike against the Turk, had taken place on the only ground where the two rival houses could have met in safety and without loss of prestige, namely, on British soil; the fact that an Englishman was witness to the peace must ensure its sincerity, and as friend of both parties I would settle any little difference that might hereafter rise between them. We all had lunch together, and I sent the whole lot off to Aleppo to confirm their agreement before the British Consul. They did so, and the incident, I fear, caused great annoyance to the local Government.

It was on his first visit, long before this time, that Busrawi proposed to take me over to his house (he was in winter quarters) that I might spend Bairam—the chief religious festival of the Mohammedan year—with him. Though it was inconvenient to leave the work it was clearly politic to be on good terms with the chief, so I left Lawrence in charge at Jerablus and started off with our head foreman, Hamoudi, as personal attendant, while Busrawi with four of his men made up the party. Horses were waiting for us on the far side of the river, and we rode up a wadi bed to the rolling plateau that stretches indefinitely eastwards. As we rode, a conversation that I overheard between Hamoudi and an elderly man who was Busrawi's chief house-carl gave me my first insight into Kurdish ways. Hamoudi, who comes of a sheikhly house distinguished for its piety, and is himself called "hoja," though notoriously a blot on the family's high record, began to inquire how the great Mohammedan festival was regarded by our hosts.

"You keep Bairam properly in your village?" he asked.

"Of course we do," retorted the other, "and this year, with the English effendi there, we mean to have fine doings. There will be music and dancing and such-like for three whole days without stopping."

"And how about prayers?" asked the hoja.

"Prayers?" said the indignant Kurd. "We'll knock any man on the head who says prayers during Bairam in *our* village!"

Busrawi himself made a not dissimilar remark once when jestingly I rebuked him for his unorthodox indulgence in strong liquors. "Forbidden they are," he allowed, "but we Kurds like drink, and we are Kurds first and Mohammedans afterwards."

We rode on, and about five o'clock in the afternoon reached a single black tent pitched in a hollow. Several men came out and cuffed off the great slate-grey hounds that guard the Kurd's flocks, and, Busrawi suggesting coffee, we all dismounted and took our seats on rugs and cushions in the open men's-quarters. The women made coffee and handed it out through the coloured curtains that veiled them from us: we drank and smoked and talked, and Busrawi's house-carl produced a bottle of raki in which he and the chief indulged freely. There were no signs of a move, and presently Busrawi made himself comfortable on his pillows and dropped asleep: conversation between the rest of us wore thin. At last our escort told me that as the day was hot it had been decided to dine here and go on by moonlight. In due time the tent-owner's sons brought in the felt tablecloth and spread it on the ground between us, throwing down along its edge in front of each man's place the folded rounds of bread, thin as fine cardboard and soft as linen, that serve at once as napkins and as food: then roast fowls were brought in, and rice, and crushed wheat boiled with millet, and we fell to with our fingers, our hosts hugely pleased to find that I had learnt beforehand the trick of twisting a piece of bread into a cone and scooping it full of rice and then swallowing the lot. After washing our hands and smoking a farewell cigarette with our coffee, we mounted our horses and, in the bright light of the newly-risen moon, went on towards the east.

We had ridden for two hours or more and the bottle had been passed times and again, for the night air struck chilly, when we passed close to a village, its tents but a huddle of black shadows between us and the moon, and saw close to our path a stack of light brushwood, liquorice tops and the like, collected for the people's firewood. Busrawi asked if I were cold.

". A little," I answered.

In a moment he was off his horse and had set a match to the wood-pile : a great sheet of flame spurted up, lighting up the village and turning all the grey stones that litter these barren lands into pools of rosy pink : the village dogs woke and made night hideous, and the Kurds shouted with laughter as we held out our hands to the blaze. In but a few minutes the whole pile was burnt, the flames died down, and we were again on our way.

It was nearly midnight when we breasted a long stony rise and saw beneath us, a mile away or so, one of the few builded villages of the country-side, a cluster of slender bee-hive huts whitewashed and gleaming ghostly in the moonlight. Busrawi, who by this time had drunk well,—though not so deeply as his old henchman, who was rolling in his saddle— pointed to the village.

"There's a man down there," he said, "who has the silliest name you ever heard—Shashu" ("Shashu" means "Ethiopian" in the tongue of ancient Egypt); "and what's more, he's got the funniest-shaped head you ever saw! You would like to see his head!"

The escort began to laugh.

"Let's wake him up!" cried the sheikh, and in a trice the horses had been spurred to the gallop and we were dashing down the rocky slope yelling, "Shashu, Shashu!" as loud as we could yell. Then as we drew nearer, Busrawi pulled out his revolver and shouting, "Shashu, get up, get up, you misbegotten

A CHIEF OF THE KURDS

son of an unnatural father; get up, we want you!" started blazing away at the village: all followed suit, shouting and shooting in every direction. As we rode up to the first house Shashu himself came running out to see what the uproar was, and at that moment the drunken henchman, galloping ahead, seized him by the back of the shirt, which was his only garment, and dashed through the village street dragging his victim with him.

"Ah, Shashu," he shouted, "you've got to see us home!"

Our horses were winded and we were weak with laughter: for my own part I was thankful to have reached the level ground without a stumble, and we slackened our pace, the luckless Shashu still being pulled along ahead of us, hardly able to keep his feet. Before we had gone far, however, he recovered his scattered wits and saw the joke; then, catching hold of his tormentor's foot, he heaved him neatly out of the saddle, jumped up himself, and, seizing the old man by the hair, dragged him along in his turn amid the renewed laughter of us all; fortunately we had only two or three miles more to go, but, tired as I was, I was not so glad to dismount before Busrawi's door as was the grey-haired old reprobate to stop running.[1]

I slept in the guest-chamber, a long room down

---

[1] I had the privilege later of seeing Shashu's head, and it was certainly odd. He belonged to a small clan which practises artificial malformation of the skull. The head and shoulders in infancy are tightly strapped against a board so that, when the process is complete, the back of the head rises in a flat disk from the nape of the neck to the abnormal peak above.

whose either side were spread thick mattresses and quilts of satin embroidered with tinsel thread. When I woke the dancing had already started on the beaten floor outside: a long pipe and a drum supplied the music, and the dance was of the usual type, a row of men shuffling their feet and clapping hands in monotonous rhythm. After the early coffee Busrawi came in and sat beside me on the dais and received the annual homage of his headmen; his elder brother first, then his sons, and then the other chiefs came in and, bending low, touched his foot and placed his hand upon their heads, wishing him the good things of the feast: the same honours were paid to myself by way of courtesy. Then we went out to watch the dancing. Busrawi's eldest son, a rather dull-witted youth with no ideas beyond sport, was here in his element and led the dancers for hours together: sometimes it was a sort of march, the leader waving a handkerchief and setting the pace as he led his line in and out as along the paths of a maze; sometimes they formed a ring with the musicians in the centre, and these would move about and then, stopping at some point in the circle, would lean forward, and with redoubled noise and gestures encourage the dancers there till they leaped high in the air, twisting and writhing like men possessed, yet ever keeping time with the soberer shuffle of the main body. I must confess that the thing grew wearisome in time. Busrawi's second son, a keen-faced clever boy of about fifteen, had been told off to look after me, and he did his duty well; no sooner had I finished a cigarette than he had rolled another, lighted it himself, and, once satisfied that it drew properly, had handed it gravely on to me. At the door of the inner courtyard was a great mud oven where two men kept the fire going and the coffee-pot ever on the boil: the little cups with their spoonful of bitter black coffee were passed round without ceasing—I drank forty and then gave up counting in despair. At last lunch came—an admirable meal—and then more dancing till dinner. At meals the sons of the house waited on us, according to tradition, retiring afterwards to share what we left with the house-servants: Busrawi and I, Hamoudi and three other Kurdish guests sat round the huge copper tray whereon were brought in all together the various dishes—lamb roasted whole and stuffed with truffles and chicken-liver, pilau, soup, fowls stuffed with pistachios, stewed apricots, stuffed tomatoes and stuffed cucumbers, ground rice, very sweet and flavoured with cinnamon, pickles and cream and dried plums—all lay before you at once and you took them in what order you pleased. Busrawi pointed out the great advantage of this system over the European one of separate courses, whereby, as he complained, the dish you liked best was snatched away before you had had half enough, and you were obliged out of politeness to eat things that you didn't like at all. Really there is something to be said for his view.

After dinner came music, and this proved an unexpected treat. Instead of the monotonous accompaniment of the dance, we had a trio of small drum, long wooden pipe, and a queer five-stringed zither, very sweet and mellow in tone, and there was an old man who sang. The four musicians squatted against the wall of the room in the harem where we had dined, guests and house-servants flocked in, and soon thick tobacco-smoke dimmed the light of the one lamp : it was an extraordinary scene, the crowded figures crouched upon the rugs, their brilliant garments making splashes of barbaric colour amid the heavy shadows, and their wild lamp-lit faces working with emotion. The music was quite unlike any Turkish or Arabic music that I have heard : it had the same minute subdivision of the octave which is so difficult a thing for any but the Oriental ear to seize, but it was as natural as the song of birds and full of little phrases and harmonies that reminded me somewhat of Hungarian music. There was a "pastoral" of really remarkable beauty, a solo by the flute with occasional accompaniment: Busrawi whispered to me the motives—"here he reaches the pastures and the wind is strong amongst the stones . . . here he sits in the sun and plays a love-tune . . . here evening comes and he calls the scattered goats together for the home journey . . . " but the comments were hardly needed, so clearly did the pipe tell its own tale. Then there was the "Lament for Hussein Ahmed." Hussein was a Kurdish Rustum, a mighty hunter, and a doer of great deeds in war, and in return for some exploit he won the hand of a princess, daughter of a sultan in some country far from his own. And as he rode homeward with his bride through a mountainous land covered with forest, there appeared amongst the trees a wolf, a bear, and a lion, and it seemed that these would fight together. But then there came from the wood a small black beast and it fought all three, the wolf first, then the bear, and lastly the lion, and overcame and slew them all. And the bride watched all this and then turning to her new lord she mocked him and said, "Thou hast killed wolves and bears and lions and many men, but darest thou fight with the small black beast yonder?" So Hussein Ahmed got off his horse and left the princess there and went into the wood and fought with the black beast and in the end he overcame it; and as it lay dying on the ground he came close to thrust it through with his sword, but the beast, in its last agony, kicked him and sent him flying through the air and crashing against the branches of the trees, and he was left hanging dead in the branches. So when she saw what was done, the princess went into the forest and took down the body of her husband, and she sang the "Lament for Hussein Ahmed," and she threw herself over a cliff in the forest and died. It is a wild song of passion with a long-drawn sob, almost a gasp, as burden to every verse: the old man sang it in a sweet voice, not too strong for the narrow room wherein we were; the audience bent and swayed with the growing anguish of the words, and broke into a low sigh with each recurrence of the refrain.

After that, the tribal march, a modern piece, sounded a poor thing.

The next two days were a repetition of the first, save that I escaped some of the dancing and rode over to call on Busrawi's elder brother, who lived a mile and a half away, and to visit some old caves in a distant hill. A Roman sarcophagus of beautiful rose-pink marble, decorated with carved garlands, formed the drinking-trough of the village herds and spoke of a more civilized past. The caves proved to be Byzantine rock-cut tombs of the usual type, square chambers with lateral niches for the coffins, but I could see no inscriptions nor anything of interest. Indeed my visit palled on me a good deal, and I was not sorry when it came to an end, interesting as it had been to get even a passing glimpse of the Kurdish life. But though during my visit I saw probably the best side, one or two things even so reminded me that my hosts were primitive savages at heart. I noticed that one of the house-servants was nursing a wounded arm and asked how the hurt had been incurred: with great glee they told me that this fellow was one of three whose duty it was to impart to Busrawi's eldest son practical lessons in the gentle art of robbery by night; a few nights before the teacher had shown how things ought *not* to be done by giving the alarm and getting a bullet-wound from the householder. A society in which the polite accomplishments of a gentleman are so catholic cannot be considered to have reached a high level. Again, being hard up for a subject of conversation, I remembered that at

A CHIEF OF THE KURDS

Jerablus Busrawi had described to me a stone about whose value he was curious, and I suggested that he should show it to me. The stone was produced, a small amulet carved in pale jade: I told him that it was not of any value and asked him where he had got it.

"Oh," said he, "it was on a gold chain between two turquoises; that's what made me think it might be valuable."

"And where did you get the gold chain?"

"Well, that was round the neck of a foreign woman we killed here a little while back." And the chief was not a whit abashed.

On our way back to Jerablus Hamoudi and I were escorted by the sheikh's younger son, a boy friend of his, and the same old house-carl who had attended us on our way out. We rode across country in the bright early morning, the boys insisting on showing off their mounts by challenging us to races, when the leader in the chase would swerve sharply to right or left, shooting his revolver in the air or throwing up his head-rope and trying to catch it again while still at the gallop. It was not bad fun at first, but racing over those stony pastures on a native saddle loosely girthed, and with nothing but a rope halter, is parlous work for the new-comer, and I was not sorry when Hamoudi took a heavy toss and expressed a strong desire for quiet going. Passing a mound whereon a few broken foundations showed above ground, I got off my horse to have a closer look; the ruins were of no interest at all—the site of some village deserted perhaps a century before, but my eye was caught by a new-made grave. Now a way-side grave usually means a violent death, the victim being buried where he is found, so I turned to the old Kurd and remarked that this one looked very fresh.

"Oh yes," he said, "the man was only killed about ten days ago."

"Who was he?" I asked.

"I don't know exactly, but he was a stranger, an Arab of sorts, who was keeping goats here."

"And how did he die?"

The Kurd chuckled. "That's a really funny story," he said. "It was this way. Two men came out to see what he had on him, and one of them hid here behind the well-head and one behind the big stone yonder; the Arab was hereabouts. Well, the man behind the well-head fired first and missed—it was a shocking bad shot—and the Arab started to stalk him round and round the well-head. But the joke of it was," and here he laughed aloud, "that he never saw the man behind the stone, so *he* got him as easily as could be!"

I looked at the old scoundrel, who was shaking with merriment. "You seem to know all about it," I remarked.

"Of course I do!" he cried. "I was the man behind the stone!"

A few days after my return to camp a Kurd drove up to the house a donkey bearing the guest-presents from my late host—a fine "killim" or woven hanging, a Persian rug which one of the sheikh's house had captured in war nearly two hundred years ago, and the coat of chain mail and steel battle-mace last used by Busrawi's grandfather. It is a point of etiquette to take such presents and to make a full return in kind, and I had been duly informed as to what would prove acceptable in the chief's eyes, to wit, two revolvers and a safety razor! These were sent back by the messenger, and I think that both sides were satisfied with the exchange.

One object which Busrawi showed to me, but to the obvious relief of himself and his family I refused to accept, was a curtain of black damask which once hung in the great mosque of the Prophet's tomb at Medina. It had formed part of the loot carried off by the Wahabis when in 1805 these Puritan iconoclasts of Islam sacked the sacred city. When Ibrahim Pasha, son of Mehemet Ali of Egypt, determined to lead an expedition into the Hejaz and punish the Wahabis, he called in the Milli-Kurds to his aid,[1] and amongst those who answered to the summons was Busrawi's great-grandfather; after one of the fights, in which the schismatics were routed and their camp taken, the Kurd found and kept this trophy of the Holy Place. The curtain was a beautiful example of Egyptian weaving, and I could not help expressing my admiration of it, whereupon Busrawi as in duty bound offered it to me, but I knew that as

---

[1] The Milli-Kurds joined Ibrahim Pasha again in 1832, when the Egyptian armies marched north through Syria, crossed the Taurus, and wellnigh destroyed the power of Turkey.

an infidel I could not take it without giving umbrage (indeed the harem was still screaming over the scandal of my even seeing it), so I told the chief that it was better left in the keeping of so good a Moslem as himself!

About the steel battle-mace a story is told that shows Busrawi's sense of humour. One of the first acts of the Young Turk Committee on their coming into power was to forbid the carrying of firearms. After Ibrahim Pasha's death the Milli-Kurds had no wish to incur by disobedience the further hostility of the Government, and Busrawi having business in Seruj, the seat of a Turkish Kaimmakam, was divided between his anxiety not to give offence and his shame at going unarmed amongst the Osmanlis. He hated the Young Turks and had good cause to mistrust the "liberty" which they preached, but he could not defy them. So when at the head of his retinue he rode into the courtyard of the Seruj serai and the Kaimmakam and his officials came out to do honour to the great man, they saw the steel mace dangling at his wrist by its cord of coloured silk.

"Mashallah, Busrawi Agha," exclaimed the Kaimmakam, "what is this?"

Busrawi tossed the mace aloft and caught it. "This is the Kourbash of Liberty!" he said. It was the story of Rehoboam over again: the whip of the old regime had become the deadly bludgeon of the new.

But the chief could turn a compliment as deftly. 1 was dining with him once and, remarking with

A CHIEF OF THE KURDS

justice on the excellence of the meal, asked who was his cook. He told me that his sister was responsible. "Good," I replied, "Busrawi, I shall marry your sister." The Kurds who were at meat with us looked up horrified and angry, for loose though they may be in the Faith, yet for a Christian to suggest marriage with one of their womankind is an insult not easily to be brooked. But the chief smiled.

"I'm afraid it is impossible," he said quietly.

"But she is an excellent cook," I insisted, "and I want to marry her."

"It is quite impossible."

As the other men looked angrier than ever I was determined to see the jest through, so "What makes it impossible?" I asked.

With the utmost gravity Busrawi replied, "It is written in the Koran that a man may not marry his brother's sister."

There was a shout of laughter from the audience, in which the chief and I joined: but I was always known thereafter as "the elder brother of Busrawi."

I have remarked before that the Kurdish women enjoy far more freedom than do their Turkish sisters, more even than the women of the Arab villages, though the latter are not ill-off in that respect: they will talk freely with the men, unveiled, and carry on village flirtations in truly European style. At the same time, their morals compare very favourably with those of Western women: prostitution, outside the great towns, is unknown, and adultery is very rare. I asked Busrawi whether the latter ever occurred, and while admitting that cases were known, he assured me that they were few and far between: "as a matter of fact," he added, "there was an instance only a little while ago in a distant branch of my own family, but it was soon dealt with." Pressed for details, he told me that his kinsman's young wife had run away with a man of another tribe: the alarm was given, and the injured husband and his relatives started in pursuit, chased them down river for a hundred and twenty miles, and caught them in a village whither they had fled for sanctuary. "And what did you do to them?" I asked. "We shot the man at once." "And what about the woman?" "Oh, we dealt with her in the way proper for such." "Which is—?" "We cut her in half and burned the two halves. But really, adultery is very rare amongst the Kurds."

Quite apart from the deterrent, which is severe enough, the ease of divorce is a great safeguard. The man has only to say three times "I divorce you," the woman has only to go off to her own family and remain there, and the marriage tie is broken. Yet divorce is not common. With the Kurds as with the Bedouin a wife is purchased from her family for cash paid down—hence the guardianship of a marriageable girl is a distinct asset—but this payment is calculated less by the maiden's charms than by her possessions and prospects. The bride will bring with her a dowry according to her station

A CHIEF OF THE KURDS

in jewellery and in household furniture: moreover, on a man's death his property is divided in set proportion between his sons and his daughters, the latter having a legal claim on the estate, and the daughter of a wealthy house is therefore a good investment. But should a man divorce his wife he must send her home with all the dowry intact that she brought with her, which he is naturally loth to do: and should she divorce him her family must return the whole of what he paid as purchase-money, money maybe spent long since and certainly not to be unearthed without reluctance, and the wife's family therefore will be all for reconciliation. A good deal of stigma too attaches to the divorced party; so that an erring or an unkind husband can nearly always be brought to reason by, at worst, a temporary flight, and a repetition of the divorce formula is seldom needed to reduce a shrew to silence.

How punctilious is Kurdish honour where their women are concerned was illustrated by an incident that occurred in our own work and caused us no little anxiety. One morning the village hoja came down to the diggings in a state of the utmost alarm, and drawing Lawrence to one side begged him to send one of our workmen, Yasin Hussein by name, up to our house at once with orders to remain there; otherwise, he declared, there might be bloodshed at any moment. Lawrence sent the man up forthwith, and then, with him in sanctuary, we started inquiries. Yasin was an Arab of Jerablus, a young fellow, good-looking in a rather effeminate way, and a dandy with no small conceit of himself: he had been carrying on a mild and perfectly harmless flirtation with a Kurd girl living in the village with her two brothers, who were also engaged upon our work, but he was not in a position to marry and had taken the little affair very lightly. The two brothers, acting as the girl's guardians, had destined her for marriage with a man of their own people, a desirable *parti* from their point of view, which was the amount that he would pay for her, but by no means to the taste of the lady. The feelings of a well-conducted girl would not have entered into the matter, but this one was headstrong and had set her heart upon the beau (who really was only amusing himself), and that very morning after the men had started off to work she had gone into Yasin's house, where his mother and sister were, and flinging herself on the ground had declared that she would marry him and no one else.

Judged by Kurd standards this was an insult put by Yasin upon the girl's family which only his death could wipe out, and sure enough the news of the outrage had no sooner reached the diggings than the injured brothers were hunting for the culprit to have his blood. I sent for them and tried to smooth things over, but they would listen to nothing: I could only tell them that if they shot Yasin without my permission I should certainly shoot them, and so cleared them out of the place. Yasin Hussein passed the night in our house, but the next day things looked still more serious. If Yasin were

A CHIEF OF THE KURDS

killed, this would at once start a blood-feud between the murderers and his family, which was a large one: in fact, at least seven villages were involved on his side, and it seemed probable that the Kurds would be supported by the whole of their tribe—which was Busrawi's—and that thus the escapade of a silly girl might lead to a regular racial war. A deputation of the sheikhs of the seven villages waited on us that day and begged us to mediate in the quarrel.

So I sent for the two brothers, and in the presence of the sheikhs made my suggestions. I pointed out that the last thing the Kurd chiefs wanted just then was a quarrel with the Arabs, and that therefore there must be no bloodshed. Yasin was to marry the girl (for nobody else would have her now), and the purchase-money would be found by the sheikhs, his relatives, who might recover from him later if they could: I fixed the price of the bride at seventy-five purses *plus* ten purses as solace-money for the irregularity of the proceedings. The two brothers had quieted down since the previous day, and after many protests accepted the ruling. I ordered the sheikhs to start payment at once.

But the following afternoon came bad news. Some of the money, in cash and in kind—sheep, goats and a horse—had been taken to the Kurds' house, but they had gone back on their agreement and returned the goods, saying that nothing short of Yasin's life would satisfy them. I sent for them again and told them that this time they had put a shame upon myself, and that if they did not submit to my ruling I should myself take up the quarrel against them. They showed clearly enough that they did not like this, but argued that to give Yasin what he had always wanted was but a poor way of avenging the insult to them, and that the insult was too great to be atoned for by the mere fact of his marrying their sister,—in fact, they would still have to kill their brother-in-law to uphold the family honour. I said "All right, then we will so closely unite the two houses as to make a blood-feud between them impossible: Yasin shall marry the Kurds' sister, as arranged, but also Yasin's sister shall marry the elder Kurd; the latter bride must bring her dowry in full, but there is to be no payment for her."

This suggestion took everybody by surprise, and it certainly would have solved the difficulty, as all admitted, though the Arab deputies did not relish the idea of their paying for Yasin's bride and the Kurd getting his gratis: but the elder brother raised the objection that he had one wife already and neither wanted nor could afford to keep a second. "Very well," said I, "then your brother shall take her; it's all the same to me." But the younger brother maintained that he had no desire to marry, and—with more point—that Yasin's sister was really too young and not at all nice-looking: "Have you seen her?" he asked pertinently, and I had to acknowledge that the objection was a fair one. So I went back to the original proposal and

A CHIEF OF THE KURDS

tried to enforce that, but the Kurds were sullenly obstinate; they now said that they dare not, after such an outrage, agree to peace on any terms without the approval of their tribal chief. This annoyed me, partly because Busrawi was in Aleppo and could not be got at without a delay which I was anxious to avoid, and my relations with him quite justified my acting in his place, but still more because, as I told them, the affair was one dealing with their womenkind, in which the tribal chief had no right of jurisdiction: but since they had appealed to the Sheikh, I said, the case should be reserved for him, and they were to keep the peace, —and to absent themselves from the diggings—until his return. This they agreed to do.

On Busrawi's arrival at Jerablus I laid the matter before him and called up his two followers for the judgement. Busrawi cursed them in unmeasured terms for not having accepted my ruling,—all the English, he said, had a right to authority over all the Kurds, and I in particular as his brother could lay down the law for his tribe. So Yasin Hussein was to marry the girl who loved him, but to punish her brothers' contumacy the purchase-money should be reduced to sixty purses, "and since you have chosen to call me in without cause," he added—for the Chief has a keen eye to the main chance as well as a sense of humour—"you shall pay a sixth of that to your Sheikh!" The brothers had to apologize humbly: and I believe that the marriage has proved a happy one!

I have already remarked that the Kurd has a strong love for money and no scruples as to how he gets it. This may be due in part to the fact that, where barter is common, coin of the realm is generally scarce; and a Kurd's wealth consists of his livestock, whereof he only sells enough to procure the few luxuries which he must needs get from the towns. A chief, therefore, who collects his tribute in kind, but has greater calls than others on his purse, may well be hard put to it at times to find ready cash; Busrawi certainly never let slip a chance of earning an honest—or a dishonest—penny (there is, by the way, no such thing as dishonesty when enemies deal together, though you should not cheat a friend), and he saw just such a chance when he ran up against the Germans.

The Kurds viewed with distrust and dismay the coming of the Bagdad Railway, which runs right across their territory; they feared the advance of civilization in general and the coming of the Germans in particular. But though they are so far beyond the reach of the law that no Turkish soldier in uniform would venture alone across their steppes, or if he did would not return from them, the chiefs dared not resist the power of the Turkish Empire backed by German authority; they decided not to oppose the railway, but to make what they could out of it.

The temporary wooden bridge across the river at Jerablus had been finished and the railhead was at Arabpunar some thirty kilometres on, when the demand for ballast for the line became urgent: for a certain

A CHIEF OF THE KURDS 217

distance from the Euphrates shingle from the riverbed was used, but beyond the point where the cost of transport made this impossible new sources of supply had to be sought, and the Germans decided to avail themselves of crushed basalt. They selected for this purpose a basalt outcrop which stood up in the form of a rugged hill a few miles away from the line near Arab-punar, and they gave out the contract for the mining and crushing of the rock to a German-speaking Salonica Jew who was doing a good many jobs for the Company. Now when building their railway from Aleppo to Jerablus the Germans had shown the least possible regard for the rights of local landowners. In defiance of the terms laid down by the Turkish Government, compensation for the expropriated land had not been paid even now when the line was already open to traffic, and the repeated claims therefore had been postponed indefinitely; they expected to pursue the same economical course east of the Euphrates, and so the quarry was chosen and the crushing machinery installed without any with-your-leave or by-your-leave put to the presumed owner. But this hill stood on the edge of the long valley at whose opposite ends lay the houses of Busrawi and of the brothers Shahin Bey: they waited till all was in place, and then, bringing up their armed men, drove off the workpeople and effectually stopped all progress.

The news came to me in the form of a pathetic letter from the Jewish contractor, begging that I should use my influence with the Kurds to allow the work of the railway. Rather puzzled as to what this meant, I sent a note to Busrawi and asked him to come and see me: in due course he appeared with the two Shahins and explained matters; their object, he said, was not to stop the work altogether, but to get compensation before it started, wherein they were acting strictly within their rights as defined by law, and they were now going to Aleppo to see the contractor and to insist on immediate payment; they suggested two hundred and forty pounds as a fair indemnity. Remembering the tone of the Jew's letter, I remonstrated and pointed out that the hill was an absolutely barren rock that never had been and never would be of any use to the Kurds.

Busrawi smiled and agreed that it was quite useless.

"But I like that hill," he said slyly. "I can see it from my house, and I like the shape of it; and Shahin Bey, who lives closer by, thinks it a beautiful hill. We can't have our pleasure spoilt for nothing."

The idea of a Kurd cultivating a taste for the picturesque was too much for my gravity; they joined in the laugh, and I sent them off with a note to the Jew advising him to pay up.

The chiefs returned with beaming faces and new cloaks, for the contractor had protested but had paid.

"So that's settled," I said, "and now the work can go on all right."

"Oh, not at all," replied Busrawi, "we couldn't allow that."

"Now look here, Busrawi," said I, "you've got to keep your word: I'm mixed up in this; I've seen that you got your compensation, and now you must do your share honestly."

The Kurd smiled. "You don't seem to understand any more than the Jew did," he said. "That hill doesn't belong to me or to Shahin Bey, *and we never said it did.* We said we liked the hill and we got paid for its being dug up; but there's the owner to consider, who's one of Shahin's men, and we are bound to see justice done to him. When he's been paid too we shall let things go on."

Sure enough there was another block, and again the Jew had to pay up; and then Busrawi was as good as his word.

On another occasion, however, the Sheikh was outwitted on his own lines. He came in to lunch with us one day looking rather glum, and explained his depression by the fact that he had got to pay some Government tax amounting to fifty or sixty pounds, and didn't like having to find the cash. We laughed at him, saying that we had not supposed he paid these taxes.

"Well, as a rule I don't," he admitted; "but this time I must, to save money."

Then the story of his discomfiture came out. Payment was as usual long overdue, and Busrawi hoped that it had been allowed to lapse, as had often happened, when one day the Kaimmakam of Seruj in person appeared at the Chief's house, together with two of his staff and a "guard of honour" of about fifty soldiers. Suspecting that this was a tax-gathering party, Busrawi had remembered a pressing engagement elsewhere, and had slipped away without meeting his uninvited guests, leaving orders that they were to be shown all the hospitality due to their rank and his own. That was a fortnight ago, but the Kaimmakam still showed not the least disposition to vacate his comfortable quarters. "I can't go home and turn them out," complained my poor friend, "for that would be inhospitable and a disgrace to myself: also it would be rather dangerous. In the meanwhile they are eating and drinking me out of house and home, and the only way to get rid of them is to pay my taxes." In justice to Busrawi it must be said that he quite saw the joke against himself, and joined in our merriment. But that year the Turkish Government got its money.

The problem of the Kurd tribes would undoubtedly be a hard one for any Government to solve. The first and most obvious step is to settle them on the land; but they have themselves not the least desire to give up their nomad life, whose freedom they are never tired of praising, nor are they the kind of settlers to reclaim the neglected steppes, for they are not by nature industrious, and when they work do so capriciously and without concentration; moreover, to develop the riches of their country would only be giving them facilities for corruption, for the vices of civilization, as we understand it, appeal to them more strongly than

A CHIEF OF THE KURDS

do its virtues. It is indeed difficult to see what part or lot they could have in a modern State, and perhaps after all the best course to adopt with them is that of the Turk, to leave them alone so far as may be to live their lives in their own way. The re-establishment of the old confederacy under one of Ibrahim Pasha's house, and a strict delimitation of frontier, at least upon the north and west, would probably be the best safeguard against active trouble; but to make "good citizens" of the Kurds is a task which would tax and overtax the powers of any one rash enough to undertake it.

NABOTH'S VINEYARD

I AM no lover of the Turk, and cannot join in those panegyrics which have been so often chanted in praise of "the finest gentleman in Europe." The Turkish peasant is a decent enough fellow—as are peasants nearly all the world over: he has the good qualities of those who live close to the soil; he is industrious, patient, wonderfully amenable to discipline, good-tempered as a rule, and withal of a more cheerful disposition than his hard life would seem to warrant; on occasion, too, he can be an incarnate brute. But Turkey claims to be a civilized and a great power, and by the degree to which she makes good that claim must she be judged. Armenian massacres and the persecution of Greek Ottoman subjects might of themselves suffice to damn the ruling class that orders them; but these things do not stand alone, they are only more glaring examples of Turkey's utter inability to understand the rudiments of what civilized government should mean. The Turks have never outgrown the stage of conquest. They ceased long since to add by force of arms province to province, and to extend the dominions of the Crescent; but just as the first inroads of the Tartar hordes had loot and sack as motive and as sequel, so to-day the Turk looks upon power as a means to self-enrichment, and regards the alien peoples of his empire not as fellow-subjects but as enemies for his plundering. I know little of Turkey proper, of the Anatolian highlands where the Turk is at home and the governing class have to deal with people of their own kith and kin; but in the provinces, where he is set as a stranger in authority, he is an unmitigated curse.

Of course, there are individual exceptions to the rule, such men as Jellal Pasha, Vali of Aleppo in 1913, well-educated, honest and well-intentioned; but even these are out of sympathy with the people they have to govern, and their best efforts are thwarted by their associates and ministers. The hopelessness of doing much real good, and the fear of those slanders which find so ready a hearing at Stamboul, reduce the best of such men to a policy of harmless inaction; and the worst, who form the vast majority, have no incentive to well-doing, and fear no sanction for its opposite: extortion, corruption, and violence are their most coveted perquisites of office.

North Syria is perhaps particularly unfortunate, for lying as it does on the fringe of Turkey proper, its population of Arab, Turkman, and Kurd is leavened with a number of resident Turks over and above its share of officials and place-holders. Now one relic of the old conquering Tartar spirit is an inordinate land-hunger, and this appetite in people whose race sets them in the eyes of government above their neighbours is for the latter a very dangerous thing. This is, or was, a country of peasant proprietors. Most Arab families own sufficient land for their own needs, land which has been handed down from father to son, and, ill-cultivated as it is, yet suffices for the wants of the household, seeing that the population increases but slowly. But if you were to compare the original Land Register drawn up thirty years ago with its present entries you would find changes which affect the whole economy of that countryside. Landlordism on a large scale is fast ousting the small-holder, and entire districts are passing into the hands of a small number of wealthy men. The change is not so apparent on the surface of things, for in very many cases the family of the old small-holder is still resident and working as tenants on the land they have lost; but in reality it has gone even deeper than official records show, for many who still by the letter of the law retain their little farms do so only on the sufferance and at the convenience of their virtual lords. Prominent above the flat roofs of many an Arab village you will see the stone house of the Turkish effendi. Probably this man will own a good half of the land belonging to the village, and may have large properties besides in the neighbouring hamlets; the villagers may still for the most part possess land of their own, but through debt or other mischance they have so fallen into the power of the big landlord that they owe him unpaid service for so many months of the year, and for that period are little better than his serfs. This state of things does not depend on any old feudal tradition, but is the modern outcome of the Government's favouritism to the Turk and absolute disregard of native rights or interests.

If this were all, there would be no need for any great outcry: but the worst feature of it is that the system of aggrandizement by alien and often absentee landlords is still spreading, and no Arab small-holder is safe from it. I have often asked an Arab—and that, too, in villages where as yet no Turkish effendi has installed himself—why he did not do more to improve the land he owned. The answer has always been the same,—he dared not, if he wished to keep it. The soil may be deep and fertile, capable, with irrigation (which in the valleys is often an easy matter), of yielding two fine crops a year: yet the owner will but scratch the surface with his wooden plough, sow the exhausted seed that has been the same for generations, and if the spring rains give the expected harvest will let his land lie fallow till the winter. If the rains fail, and only then, he will clean out his ditches or set his water-wheel to work and so win an autumn crop: but he never tries to raise much more than will pay the tax-collector and leave enough over to keep his household in food until the following year. Very little corn from these small farms finds its way to market: the ground is only asked to yield a tithe of what good husbandry would make a normal crop. Did landlordism change this state of things and result in the proper cultivation of the soil it might as a system stand excused: but it does nothing of the sort. When an effendi has grabbed a new piece of land he has not the least desire to sink money in its improvement. He instals a tenant, or employs the former owner as such, on terms that yield him income without outlay. Generally the conditions are that after Government taxes have been paid and next season's seed-corn set aside, the landlord and the tenant divide the rest of the harvest on some scale fixed between them: the landlord has as a rule sufficient interest and ready cash to prevent the overcharges with which the tax-gatherer was wont to fleece the small-holder, and so the old yield is good enough to meet the new needs. The farmer can make so little for himself that he has no incentive to harder work, the landlord is at once too niggardly and too idle to insist on the double cropping of the soil; just as the Osmanlis grasped at an empire, and in five hundred years have not stirred a finger for its material betterment, so at heart the individual Turk is more anxious to own the land than to make a fortune out of it. Thus the small-holder, while he owns the land, is afraid to improve it, and things are no better when it is taken from him.

What is the danger? You have only to find out by what means these effendis have thus recently acquired their estates to understand how real it is and how easily evoked. Suppose an Arab owns some ten or fifteen acres of low-lying land on which he labours with his sons, the women-folk helping at the harvest, and suppose that he has so worked it as to make it rather better than his neighbours' and to draw the attention of some Turk, the landlord in a village hard by, or a town merchant who would fain raise himself to the effendi class. Then the sordid little play begins.

The Turk may offer to buy, and his offer naturally be refused, or he may lie low and bide his time. The harvest is gathered and the grain heaped on the threshing-floor, but it must not be removed thence until it has been assessed by the Government tax-collector who will come his rounds to collect the moderate $12\frac{1}{2}$ per cent due to the State. The inspector delays his coming; the price of corn is going down fast, and the Arab farmer begins to fear that his stock may suffer in quality also: both are serious considerations, for he has probably some small debts that his harvest is to pay off, and thunderstorms are bad for grain lying in the open. The inspector, prompted by the Turk, still delays until a bribe induces him to make his visit: the farmer saves his corn, but at a price. In front of the inspector the grain is divided into eight equal heaps, of which one represents the share of the State. But this share is to be paid, not in kind, but in cash, and its value is assessed by the inspector who takes for his basis the prices current in Aleppo just before the new harvest—that is, the maximum city price of the year. The Arab has not got this money—or, at any rate, does not want to part with it and thereby betray the existence of his little hoard—so must needs realize part of his crop. To help him to do so, the inspector has in his train a grain-merchant, perhaps a creature of the Turkish effendi, more often the inspector's own business partner. His offer is, of course, based on the lowest price current in the villages, where the new season's corn is at a discount: the farmer cannot possibly find another market, for no one in the district buys corn, he has no means of transport, and if he had the law forbids him to move any grain at all before the tax has been paid. Consequently he is forced to sell on the spot at the merchaht's figure, and in order to raise the sum at which one-eighth of his harvest was assessed must part with maybe the half. Perhaps when he has concluded his unwilling bargain he will find that the price agreed on was for grain delivered in Aleppo and that he is responsible for the transport: this is quite beyond his powers, but the grain-merchant will once more accommodate him — at a price; some chicanery can always be found to cheat the villager, and by the time the collector is satisfied the tax has risen in effect from the original $12\frac{1}{2}$ per cent to something nearer 60 per cent of the year's yield.

Then the effendi pays a friendly visit to the official who compiles the register for compulsory military service, and the Arab is notified that his eldest son is called up for the army. Now a man who joins the army is, in nine cases out of ten, lost to his family for good and all: the service is hated, too, in that it is for the Turkish Government: and without the eldest son the farm perhaps cannot be worked; the only thing for our farmer to do is to pay the *bedeli*, the exemption fee, of sixty Turkish pounds. Maybe he has that amount buried beneath his house floor, and must sacrifice these savings of years: if he has it not, he must borrow. Now the Turk comes forward, full of sympathy, and is willing to accommodate with a loan in return for a mortgage on the farm: an agreement is drawn up in writing, the money is paid over, and the first strand of the spider's web has been spun about the victim.

Soon afterwards the eldest son is called up as a reservist, and some forty pounds has to buy his freedom. The Turk is again willing to grant a loan, and the farmer is lucky if his obliging friend does not, to save trouble, note the two sums together on the same new mortgage while still keeping the original in his possession. The Arab knows nothing of any interest—indeed the idea is foreign to him as forbidden by his faith—but the interest mounts up all the quicker through his ignorance; I have known a man who for a loan of twenty pounds paid about ten pounds annually for seven years, and for six months of each year worked as the unpaid serf of his creditor, and at the end of that time still owed him nearly ninety pounds.[1] Then too if the Turk has, as

---

[1] This was one of my own workmen. On getting the rights of the case I sent him to the effendi with a note asking him to return to me at once all the deeds, etc., which he held against the bearer, failing which I should see to it that he died suddenly: I received and destroyed all the papers and declared the debt off.

is not infrequently the case, the control of a shop in the market-town, he will encourage his debtor to deal there on credit, and these new debts will rival the mortgage interest in luxuriant growth. This may last a year or two: if necessary, and supposing that the land be worth such outlay, the other sons may be required for military service, and the payment of their *bedeli* will plunge the farmer deeper into debt; but in any case the end is the same. The mortgage is called in and the farmer is broken: the farm is put up to auction, but, encumbered as it is, no one will bid for it but the lender: the Turk therefore gets the property he coveted for a fraction of its value (and that paid on the instalment system!) while the Arab is lucky if he be left to work as a labourer on the land of his birthright.

This, with such modifications as circumstances may advise, is the normal method of the land-grabber. A more daring way may be illustrated by a story in which I knew all the actors.

On the east bank of the Euphrates, just opposite the Kala'at of Jerablus, lies the village of Zormara. The river here runs in a gentle curve. Its main current is to the right of the bed and has cut deep into the western bank, forming earthen cliffs for some five miles above the citadel rock: on the other side the old bank that rises to the upper Mesopotamian plateau falls back in a more or less straight line and is as it were the cord of a strung bow whose arc is the river: between the water and the eastern hills stretches a long segment of flat fertile ground

NABOTH'S VINEYARD

at whose lower corner stood the village. The people of Zormara were Arabs, an isolated rearguard in a country whence the Kurdish advance had ousted nearly all of the older inhabitants: they had no landlord or sheikh, but each household possessed a strip of the rich riverine plough-land and a strip of the poorer tilth or pasture on the highlands behind the village: all these holdings were duly registered in the Land Office of Birijik.

About 1906 it occurred to the villagers that their property would be vastly bettered by a canal from the river starting at the north point of their low ground and running along the fort hills, so as to irrigate the whole riverine area for an autumn crop. The scheme was approved, and the whole village set to work: the canal was dug, some three or four miles in length, fruit-trees were planted along its banks, and irrigation channels were cut so as to water each man's plot: Zormara bade fair to be the most prosperous village of the whole river country.

Unfortunately this prosperity drew the covetous attention of one Ahmed, effendi by courtesy, a well-to-do Turkish shopkeeper of Birijik. He started operations in the usual way, and by money-lending methods acquired part ownership in three of the village holdings: no others would sell, nor did he himself wish to part with further cash. Collecting about him a goodly force of armed and landless Kurds he made a surprise attack on Zormara, defeated the villagers in a scrambling fight, and drove them with their wives and children across the river. Then he settled his henchmen in the deserted cottages and started to build a stone house for himself on the village outskirts.

After a few futile attempts to regain their homes by force of arms the evicted peasants had recourse to the law, and appealed at Birijik against their supplanter. But they were Arabs—and now poor men at that—while Ahmed effendi was a Turk. To supplement the few titles he had legally acquired, he had taken the precaution of drawing up deeds of sale for all the village lands, to which his Kurdish second-in-command had forged the signatures of the Arab owners. These deeds were legally quite valueless so long as the original entries stood in the Birijik register, but a small payment to the Kaimmakam and to the Cadi was enough to decide the case in his favour without recourse to such invidious comparisons.

The villagers, who in the meanwhile had squatted in tents near Jerablus and were busy raiding the neighbouring countryside for a livelihood, now appealed to Aleppo. There Ahmed effendi had small local interest and his bribes were insufficient to bolster up his case against the plain justice of things and the profits that the Zormarites had made out of stolen cattle: Aleppo gave orders to the Kaimmakam of Birijik that soldiers must be sent to Zormara, Ahmed effendi and his men evicted in their turn, and the original inhabitants restored. The Kaimmakam despatched the troops and wired to Aleppo that the Vali's orders had been carried out. The arrival of the soldiers seems to have taken Ahmed by surprise: he attempted no resistance but begged for time; then while his son did the honours of hospitality he himself galloped off to Birijik and saw the Kaimmakam. The sum of three hundred pounds changed hands, Ahmed effendi returned in triumph to his new house, and the troops, finding their orders cancelled, departed, leaving him in possession. In vain the villagers appealed again to Aleppo: judgement had already been given, and it stood on record that judgement had been executed; the authorities refused to reopen the case.

For some time the Zormarites were too busy collecting property from the district round to indulge in anything more than a few long-distance shooting matches across the river, and Ahmed effendi was left undisturbed. But at length they got an Aleppo lawyer to take an interest in their claim, and he, in view of Ahmed's local influence and of the undeniably bad reputation which the dispossessed villagers had now earned for themselves, decided to leave provincial justice strictly alone and to appeal direct to Constantinople. It was a good move, for the authorities there took up the matter and sent down a Commissioner to make inquiries on the spot, but, unfortunately, news of this came early to the ears of Ahmed effendi, and as the mills of Turkish justice grind slowly, he decided that he had time for a *coup*. He called his Kurds together and he razed to the ground the village of Zormara. Then with the materials he built a new village a quarter of a mile away, and on the site of the old he planted fruit trees, taken already well-grown from the banks of the canal, and dug irrigation channels for his new orchard across the foundations of the vanished houses; he shifted all the landmarks of the plough-lands, he filled up some of the branch canals and dug others; and then folded his hands and waited in confidence the arrival of the Commissioner from Stamboul.

· In due time this functionary arrived, and Ahmed effendi crossed the river to meet him. He declared that he was delighted to see the Commissioner who would at last free him from a persecution under which he had long suffered. A gang of Arabs, he protested, well-known throughout the country as thieves and evil-doers, had tried by force of arms to turn him out of his village: failing in this they had sought by every means that the corruption of local tribunals could afford to evict him by process of law from the lands that had been his and his father's and grandfather's before him; their impudent claims had worried him for years, but now the justice of Stamboul would settle the whole matter to his relief.

The Commissioner retorted that the plaintiffs seemed to have made out a very good case, and that their title-deeds were apparently in order. Ahmed effendi was first astonished and then delighted at this. Hitherto the villagers had brought against him only loose verbal charges: if now they had been so imprudent as to commit things to paper and to produce title-deeds, which must of necessity be forged, then the case was simplicity itself. "Indeed," he added, "considering that none of them have ever seen the village at close quarters, their detailed descriptions must be something of a curiosity," and he asked to be allowed to see the deeds. He saw them and laughed aloud: "It is just as I thought," he said, "but come over to-morrow to Zormara, and you will see for yourself the shamelessness of the forgery."

The next day the Commission visited the village. Where the title-deeds showed houses was a flourishing young orchard; where they showed open land stood the mud-brick houses (it is surprising how soon you can make a mud-brick house look old: but in any case the Commissioner was in no mood to look into details), and in scarcely a single point did the description tally with the actual site. The Commissioner was furious at having made his voyage for nothing, and was glad to abandon so unprofitable an inquiry for the comforts of Ahmed effendi's hospitable house and to receive a *solatium* for the trick that impudent brigands had played on the Supreme Court.

Ahmed effendi is still Lord of Zormara.

ALEPPO

ALEPPO is one of the oldest, the largest, and the most picturesque cities of Turkey. Coming in by the French railway from Rayak, you climb a low rise that had bounded your horizon and see the town lying in a shallow, saucer-like hollow whose rim of rounded hills is broken to north and south by the valley of the Kuwaik River. High above its close-built houses of white or grey-weathered stone rises the Mound capped with the rust-red Castle ruins, and clear of its outskirts on the nearest hillside a great Dervish "teke" or monastery with graceful minarets and dark secular pines stands out boldly against the grey-green slopes of stony pasture; northwards a broad band of fruit orchards and gardens winds along the stream and fills all the valley bottom, where green shade, the murmur of running streams, and the droning music of the waterwheels give welcome refuge from the sweltering streets.

The railway skirts the saucer-rim to a station built outside the town against the hill's foot, and hence you will be driven past the ugly new suburb, across the Kuwaik, here a dwindled and a dirty stream, to the only hotel professing Western comforts, or up a long straight and hideous street to the Konak by the Castle moat. The town which from the railway carriage window looked so splendid seems in this first drive to have lost all its glamour, but in truth these bastard European houses and half-built shops, the pride of the Aleppine, are but the modern blot on a still lovely Oriental city: pay off your ramshackle cab and plunge on foot into the native quarter and you will forget the monstrous "improvements" of the West End in wonder and in delight.

The bazaars of Aleppo are an unending joy. If from the airy ramparts of the Castle you look down upon the city spread map-like at your feet you will be surprised to see, hemmed in by crowded roofs, a wide stretch of meadow where goats and cattle pasture, a meadow broken here and there by square sunken wells and dome-like mounds, and by slender minarets which spring like builded poplars from the grass. This seeming meadow is the roof of the bazaar. Go down through the streets and pass under a massive archway with iron-studded doors and ponderous bars, and you will find yourself in a maze of cobbled lanes bordered with booths and roofed with vaults of stone. Here is coolness and a subdued light which at your first entering seems wellnigh darkness, but to the accustomed eye resolves itself into a very riot of colour. At every so many paces a small hole in the vaulting lets through a slant ray of intense sunshine to the narrow ways: the shops, open recesses with a low counter whereon the merchant sits, are brightly lit in front and run back into obscure caves whence you catch flashes of red and green and gold as the broken sunbeams chance on piles of silk or carpets, fresh garden-stuff, hammered copper ware, or jars of spices. As you pass from the bazaar of one trade to that of another you gain ever some new effect: in the cloth-market the whole alley-way is festooned with gaudily-coloured stuffs; the jewellers' bazaar has its rows of glass boxes where gold and silver trinkets gleam with flashes caught from the live coals of the goldsmith's brazier; the vegetable market is one mass of green, with crates of oranges and heaps of white and purple grapes in their season, or fat yellow melons and early apricots; the Sûk el Nahasin where the copper-smiths are at work all day long is a blaze of burnished metal and a babel of hammering: there are the glowing ovens of the cook-shops, where the counter is spread with sesame-cakes steeped in honey, and cavernous restaurants where many-coloured sherbets are served to you in tumblers full of snow. You can wander literally for miles through these vaulted alleys, and jostled by the crowd and deafened with the noise of their chaffering you will find it hard to realize that the stone roof above your head is indeed that wide field which from the Castle you saw green with grass and dotted with goats placidly at feed.

Here and there you can turn aside into a "khan" with its square courtyard open to the sky, its tree-

ALEPPO

shaded fountain in the midst, and its arcade and gallery running round the quadrangle where the wholesale merchants have their offices and the bankers sit at their tables of exchange; or through a carved doorway you may see the cloisters of a mosque with the sunlight broad and dazzling on the marble pavement, the faithful at prayer on their carpets beneath the colonnade, and the vine-covered, turban-crowned tomb of some old saint.

And then the people! Syrians in European clothes and fez, town Arabs with cloaks of thin light-tinted silks embroidered with silver, swaggering Circassians with their long black coats, high boots, and crossed bandoliers stuffed with silver-plated cartridge-cases, Dervishes with tall sugar-loaf hats of brown felt, red-slippered villagers in gaudy prints with brown *abas* and heavy black ropes over their head-cloths, driving donkeys laden with garden produce, Bagdadis with their slender "brîms" or head-ropes bound and tasselled with silver, Anatolian Turks with baggy trousers and voluminous waist-bands, Kurds from Lake Van, drovers from Samarkand or Teheran heralded by the fivefold bells which dangle from the necks of their camels whose swaying bales block the narrow streets, black-cloaked Bedouin, Jews and Persians, Afghans and Turkmans, kavasses with their gold-embroidered Zouave jackets and silver scimitars, all these and many more crowd on the cobbled ways, all with their distinctive dress and their own manner of speech; it is a kaleidoscope of colour and a mixing-pot of races.

You pass along the tunnel where the tent-makers and the saddlers sit, and through the gateway into the sudden daylight, and before you is the Castle. A huge moat with steep stone-revetted sides runs round it, and in the midst rises the mound with its coronal of mellow walls. Just in front of you, a little to the right, is the main gateway: a lofty tower four-square and with bronze-latticed windows set in carved stone frames stands rooted on the moat's bottom, and from its arched doorway springs a gossamer bridge with slender stone piles to span the ditch and join the outer gate-tower on the level beyond. The mound, which like that of Carchemish is in part natural rock and in part artificial, must have been the site of a fortress since very early days. Aleppo or Beroea was a city allied to the lords of Carchemish: a Hittite inscription can still be seen built into the wall of one of its ancient mosques, and until recently there stood in the Castle gate-tower a lion supposed to be of Hittite workmanship, which may originally have been found in the older ruins of the acropolis; but a few years ago the lion was prised out and its head broken off by an enterprising German scientist, and we have no evidence left as to the early character of the Mound. The Castle that stands there to-day was mostly built by the Saracens, who held it against the crusaders. It replaced an earlier Byzantine fort which was captured from the Christians or their Syrian rivals by a daring *coup* in A.D. 638, when, as the tale goes, a single warrior, a giant slave named Dames, climbing up over the shoulders of his comrades, scaled the walls and so availed to admit the troops of Abu Obeidah. It is still regarded as a military stronghold; soldiers guard it, and when I paid my first visit there it was a depot for Turkish army stores: in one room were the rotting remains of bows and arrows, and several vaults were filled with gun-flints. But indeed it is no more than a ruin, with only the gate-tower and the outer walls still tolerably complete, while within, mosque and bailey are but a huddle of broken walls and grass-grown hollows; yet even so it is one of the finest examples left to us of Arabic military architecture of the twelfth century, and more than anything else does its dominant bulk give character and beauty to the town.

One cannot speak of Aleppo without a word about the old houses of the Christian quarter. From narrow lanes shadowed by blank walls and spanned by frequent bridges one passes through a small double doorway into a sunny courtyard, marble-paved and gay with orange-trees and flowering shrubs; in the centre is a fountain of rose-pink or honey-coloured marble, where the water runs from basin to basin along fantastic channels and gives to the air a pleasant coolness; the door- and window-frames are richly carved, and long gargoyles, in the form of grotesque lions, threaten from the roof-edge. On one side of the court is a wide arch with coloured voussoirs intricately cut, behind which lies a square

R

open-air reception room, the selamlik, with its raised mosaic floor, its open-work balustrade, carved roof, and brightly-covered couches. Inside the house are rooms with painted panelling or curious inlay of many woods, the ceilings of eighteenth-century gilt and lacquer all a wonder of flowers and arabesques and texts in red and blue and gold. It is hard to credit that the rich families who own these glorious old places should leave them for the cramped jerry-built villas of the western suburb, but so fashion wills, and the neglected palaces are one by one falling to decay.

Beyond the castle and the open space of the camel-market stretches the Arab town. Here too, behind inhospitable-seeming walls, are exquisite interiors. You must stop outside the door and shout a warning, so that the women-folk may take refuge from the eyes of the intruding male, and only when the coast is clear may you pass into the court and so to the selamlik. Here—if you get right of entry at all, and that is none too easy—you will find lacquered ceilings and carved panelling, shelves crowded with old porcelain running round the rooms, and rich rugs on the matting-covered floors: here too are fountains and pavements of marble, black and white and *rosso antico*, and dais steps inlaid with many-coloured tiles of Damascus or of Anatolian glaze, and your coffee cup may be brought to you in holders of old filigree work, and preserved fruits in silver baskets of Selim II's time.

But I am not writing a guide-book to Aleppo,

ALEPPO

and God forbid that I should try to attract visitors to this still fairly unspoiled city of the East. I only wish to push home my indictment. Hitherto I have told of what Turkish government means in the villages of North Syria, and lest it be thought only natural that conditions should be backward and the abuse of power rife in the remote country-side, I would say something also about Ottoman rule over a beautiful and a historic city, a city whose population—put at a quarter of a million, but the figure is surely too high—is at least a large one, where business is considerable, where education is above the level normal in Turkey, but where the official class alone is Turkish, and the inhabitants, Moslem Arabs or Christian Syrians, Jews or Armenians, are all alike alien to their masters. Here if anywhere outside Stamboul, here in one of the most important towns of the Empire, the Committee of Union and Progress should have made its greatest efforts, should have installed its most enlightened officers, and justified itself by its works.

In 1912 the Municipal Council of Aleppo decided to raze the Castle, to fill up the moat with the debris of wall and mound, and on the level space so made to build a new " model " quarter with electric tramways running on an endless and an aimless joy-ride round the circle of the ditch. Quite apart from the question of vandalism, there were practical difficulties more than enough to damn the scheme, but these were never even discussed: a contract for the work of destruction was given out, and doubtless this much at least would have been done and the town's chief ornament reduced to an unsightly mass of rock and rubbish had not our urgent appeals to Constantinople resulted in an order forbidding the Castle to be touched. Another suggested "improvement" is to run a broad roadway with an electric tram-line through the heart of the bazaar; no business reasons have been adduced for this, and it might have been supposed that the terrible example of the existing main street would have prevented a second such experiment: but it means a change and a deal profitable to some one, so the scheme is only too likely to be carried out. The Young Turk reverses the sentiment of Theodoric the Goth, and in agreement with some local boards nearer home holds that the destruction of anything old is the truest progress.

But ill-judged though these projects were, they yet might seem to argue that the rulers of Aleppo are anxious after their lights to do something for the town. It is quite true that various schemes of reform have been from time to time put forward, but these, even when laudable in themselves, have only thrown into relief the hopeless inefficiency of the Turks or their corruption.

The local Minister for Public Instruction once approached me with a request which he quite clearly thought a moderate and simple one. He had started a National Public Library at Aleppo and wished me to ask the British Government to present thereto a copy of every book published in England! I told

ALEPPO

him that this was a big order, and asked what kind of works the library was to contain. He answered, every sort—history, poetry, novels, science, everything, and that in every language;—there were no limits at all to his ideas. I wondered what buildings were to house this enormous collection, but was assured that adequate accommodation had been provided already. So I went to visit the institution. I found that in the new offices of the Ministry two fair-sized rooms had been set apart, one as reading-room, the other as library proper, and in the latter a few ornamental bookcases had been installed, with a total capacity of perhaps three thousand volumes: the Minister showed me round with the greatest pride, and would not admit that his arrangements left anything to be desired or that his scheme was at all incommensurate with his space. Perhaps he was right after all, for he left Aleppo shortly afterwards, and I do not imagine that his successors would ever trouble themselves about the Library, and so the bookshelves are really not likely to be overcrowded for many years to come.

Lack of continuity is one of the great faults of the Turkish administration. One Vali, for example, is interested in roads, *i.e.* thinks that road-making will be a good source of income, so embarks on a far-reaching project, collects money by special taxation, gives out his contracts, and starts work with a flourish of trumpets. Then he is moved to another province. His successor finds that the road-contractors have already been bled for all that they are worth, and neither credit nor profit is to be got by following out another man's scheme: so the roads are left, very likely in a worse state than before the improvements were begun, and a pressing need is felt for new public buildings, for sanitation, or what not, and fresh taxation and a fresh set of contractors line the pockets of the new Vali.

At Aleppo a much-needed reform is that of the water-supply. The Kuwaik, the only stream, is well-nigh exhausted by the irrigation channels of the gardens; when swollen by winter rains it sometimes floods out the low-lying quarter of the town, but in summer it is a mere trickle of water half lost in a broad bed of mud and shingle, which below the houses is no more than an open sewer. About five miles away there is a small spring whence water is brought on donkey-back and sold in the bazaar, but the supply is scanty. For the most part the town depends on stored water. Every house has its underground cistern to catch the drainage from courtyard and roof, and these cisterns, filled by the autumn and spring rains, suffice more or less throughout the hot months; but it is a precarious and none too healthy system. One Vali tried the experiment of artesian wells. The wells were bored and towers for the windmills erected above them—low squat towers of solid stone, set in the most sheltered spots so that the delicate works might not be damaged by excess of wind. Then a difficulty arose about some part of the machinery, to whose

ALEPPO

cost the Vali would not agree. By the time the rest of the machinery was too rusty to have any value it was sold as old metal : the windmills which no obtrusive breeze had ever made to turn were dismantled, and the masonry towers were allowed to fall to gradual ruin.

But another Vali bethought him of another plan. Thirty miles or so above Aleppo, the Kuwaik runs but a few miles distant from another river, the Sajur, which has three times its volume : what more easy therefore than to dig a canal between the two, and so give Aleppo all the water it could want ? It was true that if the Kuwaik alone sometimes causes serious floods, the Kuwaik *plus* the Sajur was likely to do considerable damage in spring-time, but that was a consideration which did not bother the Turk : the town required water and it was going to get it.

So the canal was dug, and a day was set apart for the opening ceremony. In a clear space in the gardens above Aleppo grand-stands were erected, gay with crimson bunting : all the local Ministers and the whole Consular corps were invited to attend : the Vali himself was to press the button which would give the signal for the last barrier of earth to be cut away, and the Mufti was to bless the waters when they came down in a healing flood to the parched city.

It was summer and the Kuwaik was low between its banks when the guests crowded the grand-stand, the button was pressed, and the canal was opened.

All looked for the rise of the waters. For some time nothing happened, and then the anxious watchers saw the Kuwaik slowly shrinking and dwindling away before their eyes until where the shallow stream had run there was left but ooze and mud. The Turks had forgotten to take the levels, and their canal drained in the wrong direction; there was nothing to be done save to fill in the cutting and content themselves with the old inadequate supply.

Under the old regime telephones were forbidden in Turkey, as Abdul Hamid thought that they lent themselves too readily to the use of conspirators. The Sultan, though himself a good handicraftsman —I have seen beautiful specimens of cabinet-work made by him—had a rooted distrust of electricity. But since the Young Turks came into power the advantage of the telephone, at least for Government purposes, has been realized, and in 1912 it occurred to the Chief of Police at Aleppo that his various police-stations ought to be thus connected up with each other and with his central office. The scheme was at once approved by the Municipal Council, for up to that time there was no such thing as a telephone in the city, and this would mark a distinct step forward on the path of civilization.

But the suggestion that tenders should be submitted by engineering firms was strongly opposed: the Municipality urged that to employ contractors was but to waste Government money and was quite unnecessary: "The Turks," they said, "are as civilized as any one else, and have nothing to learn from others: these European inventions present no difficulties for us. The necessary plant can be purchased in Germany, and we can put it up ourselves." Such patriotism recommended itself strongly to all the members, the outfit was purchased *en bloc*, and the telephone duly installed by the Council's own workmen.

But when the Chief of Police came to test his new machine he could get no answer from anywhere. The telephone would not work. The Municipal Council met and discussed the matter: they adjourned to examine the instruments and they met again to talk, but the cause of the failure remained a mystery. At last, and much against the grain, they called in an electrical engineer, who pointed, out that whereas all else was in order the workmen who had put up the insulators had not seen the need of attaching the wires to these and so had as a rule wound them round the iron brackets or nailed them to the posts: the whole current was running to earth.

The Municipal Councillors were much disgusted at the stupidity of their workmen and soon had the oversight corrected, and once more the Chief of Police made trial of the telephone. He called up the most out-lying of his branch offices and ordered all men attached thereto to report to him at a certain hour. When the hour struck the streets leading to headquarters were packed with a seething mob of policemen from every office in Aleppo, all trying to fight their way through to their Chief: again something had gone wrong, for this time instead of no one hearing the call every one had received it.

The Council held no less than three agitated meetings to discuss the fresh fiasco, and at the third a prominent C.U.P.[1] man, who had lived long in Constantinople and had visited Germany, undertook to explain the matter. "The Council made a mistake at the outset," he declared, "in buying dry batteries: for a telephone, wet batteries are essential, and until you get these you can't possibly have any success." The Council were deeply impressed: of course that was the reason, and it was extraordinary that no one had remarked on it earlier: well, they must scrap the present batteries and get wet batteries from Germany. They did so, the Chief of Police repeated his experiment, and Aleppo again saw all its police force collected in a struggling mob round the central office. After a vain discussion and many mutual reproaches the Council threw its hand in and invoked the aid of a professional engineer. The expert pointed out that as they had only a single wire and no exchange board they could hardly have expected any other results; he offered to put in an exchange, but the Council were not going to be overridden like that by an outsider and a foreigner, and preferred to abandon the telephone.

Of all the towns I know, Aleppo is the worst paved. In the winter of 1913–14 cabs going along the new main street had to drive on the side-walk, because the roadway was too dangerous: in the space

[1] Committee of Union and Progress.

of a quarter of a mile on the only road between the city and the Bagdad Railway Station I have seen four carriages, all going to meet the same train, broken into bits in the ruts and holes: the minister responsible for the state of the streets incautiously stepped out of his cab in the principal square (the cab had stuck fast) and was nearly drowned in three feet of mud. The scandal became so crying that at last the cabmen, who found that no amount of employment repaid them for the damage done to carriage and horses, went on strike and brought traffic to a standstill.

The Municipal Council, feeling that this matter was beyond their powers, had recourse to a Young Turk, a member of the Committee, who had recently come to Aleppo: as he was a native of Beirut, had lived in Berlin, and was rather a light of the Party of Progress, they felt that he would certainly solve the difficulty and were prepared to be bound by his recommendations.

After mature thought the expert produced his panacea: it was that all drivers of vehicles for public hire should be obliged to wear khaki uniforms of an approved pattern. The idea was hailed as a stroke of genius and at once put into law, and the Council felt that they had done all that could be expected of them.

Of course there was something behind this. The men had to procure their uniforms from the local government at an exorbitant price, and the profits might have formed a nucleus for a road-repairing fund: possibly too there was a notion that the drivers, once dressed in quasi-military uniform, would not be able to go on strike at pleasure: actually, the weather being cold, the cabmen hid their khaki under civilian cloaks or overcoats and soon forgot to wear it at all, while the profits on the uniforms disappeared through the usual channels.

As the cabmen, however, seemed ungrateful for what had been done, and the condition of the streets grew worse, a new plan was devised. A famous Egyptian singer had been engaged to give a series of performances in a garden-theatre and his coming had been advertised freely. When he reached Aleppo the Egyptian was dismayed to find that his concerts were forbidden by the Government. He went to the Serai to make inquiries, and was then told that the programme might be carried out provided that he gave an opening performance the gross takings of which should be made over to the Municipality for the paving of the streets. The artist had no choice but to agree, and then the local ministers and the members of the Council assumed the rôle of ticket-sellers: they went round to the wealthy Armenians and Christian Syrians and forced them to buy seats at five pounds apiece (I saw this being done myself), and as the garden-theatre was a large one they made a very handsome sum out of their concert. No plans for the road repairs had been made, and no estimates drawn up: but three months' later a number of cart-loads of soft local lime-stone were dumped down along the main street, making it finally impassable, and the heaps were still there when I last saw Aleppo. It is worth while remarking that fine hard stone can be quarried alongside the railway at Akhterin, thirty miles to the north, and that the Municipality owns an unexploited asphalt spring not a great distance from the town.

Even worse than the main street was the principal thoroughfare of the new Christian quarter: here our Consul, returning one night from a party, saw a two-horsed carriage just in front of him disappear bodily; it had fallen into an unprotected hole twenty feet deep, and the Consul had to fetch ropes to rescue the inmates. Granted that this state of things was rather abnormal, the reason for it was characteristic. The Arab town in Aleppo is served by open drains running down the middle of the streets, an unpleasant and malodorous system, but under an eastern sun not altogether insanitary. The southern quarter, with the bazaar, is drained into a great common sewer which when not choked up empties itself into the Kuwaik and makes of that unlucky stream a noisome swamp. The rest of the town has no common sanitary system, but each house or pair of houses is built over a soakage pit: these pits are foul in themselves and the more dangerous from their proximity to the drinking-water cisterns which also lie below the houses.

The inhabitants of the street in question, one of the most aristocratic in Aleppo, appealed to the Municipality to install a proper drainage system connected up with the main sewer. The request, naturally, was refused. They then determined to carry out the scheme at their own expense, and, for a consideration, leave to do so was granted. Huge holes were dug in the road, and the intervening spaces were tunnelled: but then it was discovered that to connect with the town sewer was still forbidden and would mean more heavy expenditure in baksheesh, so some of the householders objected, and for a month or two work was stopped. Then they decided that if a proper system could not be obtained they might at least use their excavations for a common soakage-pit, which would be less noxious to their water-supply; so work was restarted. A few days later one of the labourers unearthed two or three bones at the bottom of his shaft: the discovery was reported, and the Municipality accused the Christians of desecrating a Mohammedan graveyard! Again the work was stopped while the character and religion of the bones was under discussion, and at last a final embargo was put upon the whole drainage-scheme. The householders were not going to pay out any more money, the Council denied responsibility for the state of the road, and the result is that some of the best houses in Aleppo are only to be approached gingerly and with peril over mounds of sticky earth and past yawning crevasses; at night, as lamps are few and feeble, it is a street to be avoided.

One could tell innumerable stories of such incompetence on the part of the Turks when faced with the problems of city government: every Turkish town would give material evidence of the same in streets begun well but half blocked by rubbish and ending in cart-tracks, in buildings planned ambitiously and left half-finished, in expensive machinery thrown aside to rust, in schemes promising on paper but childishly attempted or dropped as soon as money has been made by their exploitation. But it may be urged that this incompetence does not necessarily go hand in hand with corruption such as I have attributed to the Turkish officials of the great towns as freely as to their naturally more backward brethren of the outlying villages. Now, while making all allowance for an honest individual here and there, I do impute corruption to the major part, and perhaps I may be allowed to tell two stories in support of my charge: the first deals with a single officer, the second with a whole provincial government.

The Military Commandant of the Aleppo Vilayet, an official no less powerful than the Vali, received one day in 1913 a visit from a foreign antiquary, whom, as the good man is still alive, I will call Mr. X. The conversation touched on antiquities, and at once the Turk was full of a recent scandal. It appeared that a certain Baron von Oppenheim had been carrying out excavations in North Syria, and a report had reached the Government that he was not handing his finds over to them, as by the terms of his agreement he was bound to do; so when he came down country the Military Commandant had seized his luggage. The baron protested that the ninety odd packing-cases contained only the clothes and personal effects of his assistants, but they were opened and found to be full of antiquities of all sorts, so they were promptly seized. The Turkish officer was full of self-satisfaction at his capture, and of reproaches against the German, who not only had broken his agreement but was stealing Government property and robbing Turkey of her historic monuments: he seems to have waxed quite eloquent and very wordy in his denunciations. When at last the subject was exhausted he turned to Mr. X. and asked to what he owed the pleasure of his visit. Mr. X. replied that he had heard indirectly that the Commandant's son was, illicitly, carrying out excavations on a promising mediæval site: was that true?

"Certainly," replied the Turk.

"Well, as mediæval Arabic is just in my line," said the antiquary, "I hoped that if your son found anything of interest I might be the first to see it, and perhaps I might be able to buy."

The Commandant said that he would write at once to his son telling him to hold over all finds for Mr. X.'s inspection.

"But of course," pursued Mr. X., "I should want to take the things home, which might be difficult, and I could only buy if I were sure that I had facilities for getting them out of the country."

"I quite understand that," answered the Commandant, "and I will undertake that anything you buy from *us* will pass through the Customs without the least trouble."

Whether or not he kept his promise I cannot say, but his readiness to make it speaks for itself.

It was in 1911, if my memory serves me, that a certain Frenchman living in Aleppo bought a plot of building-ground on which he proposed to erect a shop. In accordance with local by-laws, all plans and specifications for the building were sent in to the Government offices, and in due time were returned to him approved, with permission to begin work on the date proposed by him. But when early that morning the Frenchman went to see things started, he found the site occupied by soldiers under a sergeant, who refused admission to him and to his workmen, and said that the building had been forbidden.

The Frenchman, much perplexed, went to the Serai, and seeing the Minister concerned, asked for an explanation: none was forthcoming, but the prohibition remained absolute. So he went to his Consul and asked him to take the matter up. The Consul saw the Minister, who deeply regretted that permission to build had been withdrawn, but insisted on its withdrawal: as he could give no reasons the Consul demanded to see the Vali, and referred the question to him. The Vali at first professed ignorance of the whole affair—probably with truth—but after consulting his subordinate, told the Consul that though the specifications were all in order, and had been approved, circumstances had since changed, and the Government had been obliged to rescind its permit. "I cannot explain it all," he said, "but it is little more than a matter of form: if your compatriot will submit his plans a second time, I have no doubt that they will be finally passed."

Then the would-be builder saw his mistake. He remembered that when he sent his papers in the first time there was one official whom he had failed to bribe: now he was being asked to make all the other payments over again, as well as to satisfy the one disappointed functionary; he explained this to the Consul.

The Consul was a strong man, and now an angry one. "You admit," he said to the Vali, "that the specifications were approved, and that permission was given to dig. I quite refuse to admit that any circumstances have arisen such as to invalidate the permit, and I insist that this gentleman be allowed to go on with his work unhindered."

The Vali politely regretted that this was impossible.

"Very well, then," said the Consul, "I shall tell my client to bring his workmen to the site at 6 A.M. to-morrow, and I shall go there myself to meet him. I shall wear uniform, and shall be accompanied by my kavasses: also, I shall be armed. If any soldier or officer sent by you attempts to stop the work being carried out, then, acting in my official capacity as representative of the French Republic, I shall shoot him on the spot. In wishing your Excellency 'good morning,' I beg you not to forget that the hour is fixed for 6 A.M."

The next morning the Consul appeared as he had promised to do, but there were no soldiers, nor was any further objection raised to the building of the Frenchman's shop; nor did the Vali ever show the least resentment for the Consul's high-handed action.

The salaries assigned by the Ottoman Government to its civil servants are low in theory, and in practice are often reduced by fifty per cent, thanks to stoppages and forced contributions to supposedly national funds: it is hardly surprising therefore that these civil servants, who have little or no sense of public duty, follow in the steps of Verres and his Roman compeers, and recoup themselves by the plunder of their provinces. In town or country alike, the Turkish official, set in authority over an alien population, is a mere beast of prey, as incompetent as he is corrupt, and as corrupt as his opportunities allow: the skin-deep civilization of the Young Turk, while leaving him just as incompetent, has but increased his opportunities, and helped to cloak his corruption. Even were it possible to reform the Turkish Civil Service, that would not avail to end abuses, for the real abuse is the fact of a Turkish Government over Arab Syria. I have seen enough of what that means to welcome any change whatsoever, if only to rid the country of that incubus which for centuries has lain so heavily upon it.

THE END

Lightning Source UK Ltd.
Milton Keynes UK
UKHW021252180220
358912UK00004B/904